WITHDRAWN

PERENNIALS
FOR THE
LOWER MIDWEST

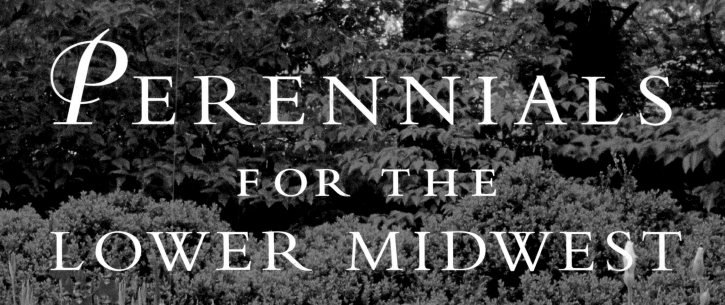

PERENNIALS
FOR THE
LOWER MIDWEST

Ezra Haggard

INDIANA UNIVERSITY PRESS

BLOOMINGTON ∽ INDIANAPOLIS

The paper used in this publication meets the minimum
requirements of American National Standard for Information
Sciences—Permanence of Paper for Printed Library Materials,
ANSI Z39.48-1984.

Manufactured in Singapore

Library of Congress Cataloging-in-Publication Data
Haggard, Ezra.
Perennials for the lower Midwest / Ezra Haggard.
p. cm.
Includes bibliographical references (p.) and index.
ISBN 0–253–33067-X (cl : alk. paper) — ISBN 0–253–21014–3
(pa : alk. paper)
1. Perennials—Middle West. 2. Perennials—Southern States.
3. Landscape gardening—Middle West.
4. Landscape gardening—Southern States. I. Title
SB434.H26 1996
635.9'32'0977—dc20   95–46331

1 2 3 4 5 01 00 99 98 87 96

Sponsoring Editor: Roberta Diehl
Book and Jacket Designer: Pamela Albert
Production Coordinator: zig Zeigler
Typeface: Bembo
Compositor: Mary Blizzard
Printer: Tien Wah Press

This book is dedicated to the Johnson girls: Georgia, Juanita, and Stella.

Contents

Introduction

In the twenty years I have been working with perennials, I have watched them gradually becoming more and more popular. Perennials, besides adding beauty to a home, increase its value. There are perennials for problem areas, and perennials that grow better and require less work than a lawn. Over the many years they survive, perennials offer more value for the money spent than anything else I can think of.

Value is the main ingredient in their rising popularity today. Once installed, they may be around for decades or longer. What is more important, whenever we look at them, they help us celebrate life in all its glory. Perennials make it easy to get to heaven. It's right there—out in the garden.

Coreopsis 'Sunray' with pink petunias.

֍

Most beginning gardeners in the Lower Midwest, as elsewhere, probably start out with annuals that they see displayed in front of the supermarket in spring. But before too long, they tire of the poor selection available and the sameness of their gardens year after year. A vast new world opens up to them when they realize that there are thousands of perennials to choose from and that perennials do not have to be planted each year.

What's so great about perennials? The huge variety of shapes, colors, and sizes that make it possible to have a garden unlike anyone else's. The fact that, if reasonably content, they come back year after year, and even reproduce. Seeing old favorites return each spring is a special pleasure. Watching the garden evolve throughout the year is another. Being able to give spare plants away to fellow gardeners is a third. And perennials make a garden a continuous treasure in a way that annuals do not, because they are present even through the winter. Although some are then dormant, others add texture and an architectural element year-round, just as trees and shrubs do.

Unfortunately, certain perennials do not like our part of the world—what Diane Heilenman (*Gardening in the Lower Midwest*) calls the "Zombie Zones." They may need evenly cold temperatures and consistent snow cover to survive the winter, or they can't handle our hot, steamy summers. You may be able to coax such plants to grow for a while, but soon they will fade away, lending truth to that old joke definition of a perennial: a plant that, had it lived, would have come up year after year.

But, while there are certain perennials that some gardeners will go to any lengths to raise, there are others that have proven over and over again to be easy and reliable, some of them lasting beyond the gardener's lifetime. For every plant that won't thrive in the "Zombie Zones," there are at least two more that will. Having planted thousands of perennials, I have learned which ones work in our area. These plants can be found in the following pages.

The purpose of this book is to provide the gardener with a reliable and interesting selection of perennials that have proven themselves in the Lower Midwest, making unnecessary the arduous task of translating possibilities from a generalized U.S. gardening book, or even one from across the Atlantic Ocean. Accompanying photographs show the plants both close up and in typical garden settings, giving an idea of scale, form, and texture as well as suggested companions.

❦

Aside from general appeal, the major criteria I have used in assembling this list are: ability to withstand both our hot summers and the alternating freezing and thawing of our winters; good-looking foliage throughout most of the growing season; extended bloom period; minimum care requirements; and adaptability to our various soil types.

I have omitted some excellent perennials such as pulmonaria and heliopsis, owing either to space considerations or to personal prejudices. I have also omitted delphiniums and roses, both of which require fairly intensive care. Roses play an important role in every garden I have designed, and I'm delighted to see their increased popularity. There was a time when I had to order "English" roses from Canada and California; now they can be found at local nurseries. I hope to cover roses in detail in a later book.

Most of these perennials will do well without extensive fussing. *Some* maintenance is necessary, or at least advisable. In a few cases, spent blossoms may be left on the plant for textural and winter interest. And, of course, if a wildflower or meadow garden is contemplated, seed heads need to be allowed to mature. Otherwise, deadheading is important to promote extended periods of blossom and a tidier appearance. Left alone, many of these perennials will flower well regardless.

Gardeners will find themselves spending more time amending the soil than they do raising plants if they allow ideal cultural requirements to dictate plant choices all the time. As a matter of company policy, I now avoid changing the existing soil texture and pH balance as much as possible. That is not to say that I don't sometimes amend the soil to accommodate a client's desire for a particular perennial, such as delphinium. But by and large, I simply choose perennials that will grow happily in the soil that is already there. Then, whether it's a small area or a large bed, I add a layer of compost, sometimes mixed with soil (or with peatmoss if changing the pH is required for acid-loving plants), directly on top of the existing soil. Once this is done, I can dig in the organic matter as each plant is installed, thus improving the soil as I go along.

Another practice which yields good results is to fertilize. I use a general fertilizer (10–10–10) twice a year—once in spring, once in midsummer— usually followed by a top dressing of compost in the fall. Fertilizing is especially beneficial if the perennials are growing in clay soils. Granular fertilizer, whether organic or a derivative, is easy to sprinkle around the crowns of established plants. After applying the fertilizer, go back and shake the plants' foliage to jar any grains that might remain there onto the ground. This prevents fertilizer burn on the leaves. When installing new plants, it's a good idea to mix granular fertilizer in the bottom third of the hole with the existing soil.

Few of these perennials have any insect problems. For those that do, I have tried to mention a satisfactory organic or relatively untoxic solution. I mainly use a preventive program of integrated pest management, which above all means careful observation so as to detect problems early, before the situation necessitates the use of highly toxic insecticides. Insecticidal soap, summer oil, Sevin (for those nasty Japanese beetles), and sulfur as a fungicide make up my arsenal. These methods—along, as I have said, with my habit of choosing tolerant plants in the first place—have proven very successful for me.

A note on spacing: In a planting that incorporates shrubs and other perennials, I usually use at least three, one to three feet apart (depending on the mature breadth of the plant) in a triangular pattern. This creates a clump large enough to make an impression. But there are no hard and fast rules, and sometimes spacing constraints or the form of the garden will dictate different shapes.

ᦉ

My list of perennials is in no way intended to be comprehensive, and without doubt there are those who will disagree with it because I have left out some of their favorites. Also, I have sometimes stretched the technical definition of "perennial" to include a couple of biennials and an annual that reliably reseed themselves year after year.

Any disagreement about some of my choices is encouraged, and I welcome comments from readers. There is always room to learn more. Gardeners, by the spadeful, are some of the most developed individualists I have had the pleasure to meet, and are always willing to share their knowledge and opinions—sometimes whether encouraged or not. I have personally enjoyed all the people I have met in the gardening world, and consider myself fortunate to be able to earn my daily bread as a garden designer, while at the same time sharing enthusiasms (OK, obsessions) with other gardeners.

Every gardener evolves differently. When I started out, my horticultural knowledge was limited, to say the least. I had just returned from Vietnam and was looking for something to do with my life. I took a job in a Lexington nursery and became fascinated by plants. Those early years were the "dark ages" of gardening; it was not a subject of general interest, and few books were available. But I began studying botany and hiking around the woods, identifying and observing the abundance of native vegetation in its natural habitat, and gradually gained a "feel" for what plant to place where. Some will tolerate a variety of places and soils; others are more particular, but if given the environment they need are perfectly happy. Eventually I had a whole new world of plants to work with and choose from, and that made life a lot easier.

My beginning is probably why the burgeoning native-plant movement comes as no surprise: I have always used native plants. Their current popularity is welcome vindication for those who have been promoting their worth all along. Numerous natives are recommended in this book.

Many indigenous plants have relatives on the other side of the world. Maples, for instance, grow in both North America and Japan. It turns out that the climatic conditions of continents on opposite sides of the globe can share similar characteristics. A study of global weather patterns reveals this, too. In my experience, plants suited to the local climate are the best ones to use, whether they be natives or not. The suitable (environmentally correct) garden can incorporate non-native as well as native plants. There are many non-natives that we have been using for centuries that work just as well for us as natives (some have been here so long most people think they *are* natives) and have not overburdened the ecological system. In short, plants most suitable for an area are native plants and those that share similar cultural requirements.

Nothing is more rewarding than succeeding with an unknown perennial, and I do not mean to discourage gardeners from trying something different or unusual. I do mean to provide a catalog of perennials that can be trusted to do well in the Lower Midwest, and with which you can create a base upon which to build a new garden or expand an existing one.

Gardening is much more fun if the results do not involve wasted time and money. With this book, I hope I will have made life a little better both for beginners and experienced gardeners who don't want to spend twenty years learning which perennials to use.

Fall scene at Burnham Woods Nursery, Bloomington, Indiana.

Allen W. Clowes

Gardeners and book lovers throughout the Midwest owe a debt of gratitude to Allen W. Clowes, a gardener and gentleman nonpareil, for the contribution which made this book possible at an affordable price.

Indiana University Press wishes to thank Mr. Clowes for his generous support.

Perennials

FOR THE

LOWER MIDWEST

The gold plates of yarrow against the bark of a Carolina silverbell tree.

Yarrow with blue spruce; lamb's-ears in the rear.

Achillea is a superb perennial for hot sun and dry soils. The large, round flat heads of yellow flowers stand out from late spring to midsummer. 'Coronation Gold', the yarrow most frequently used, has five-inch-wide plates of mustard-yellow flowers in a dense cluster, usually standing three feet tall. 'Coronation Gold' looks good with loosestrife and especially with all blues.

In the setting photo a blue spruce, *Picea pungens* 'Hoopsii', creates the background for the yellow heads of yarrow, complementing the purples and blues. A little white—*Astilbe × arendsii* 'Bridesmaid' and *Stachys byzantina* (lamb's-ears)—blends it all together.

The gray-green foliage of yarrow harmonizes with the bright yellow of the flowers. It has a wonderful ferny texture that adds to this perennial's value even after the blossoms have faded. The foliage stays around, providing interest until the end of the growing season.

Although yarrow does have the tendency to fall over after a rain, even then it fulfills its place in the planting. It can be staked if one wants to go to the trouble, but as long as it is not totally smashed down I usually don't bother.

Another advantage of yarrow is that it is not particular about soil types. The soil doesn't have to be fertile, or the best of loam. The yarrow in the photographs is growing in a well-drained but yellow clay. If you have a hot, dry, infertile spot, this is what to plant.

To add to its value, yarrow is an excellent cut flower and an easy one to dry. Hang it upside down in a cool, dry place, or simply leave it standing in an empty vase, and you will have it all winter. It does fade, but still retains some of the original yellow.

Perhaps my favorite achillea is one with a lemon-yellow blossom called *A*. × 'Moonshine'. It is brighter than 'Coronation Gold', and is less floppy than other yarrows because it is only two feet tall.

There are some recent German strains of achilleas now offered that are promising additions to the group. The Galaxy strain comes in pink to bright crimson, with a salmon pink in between. They range from two to three feet, flower brightly, and fade to luscious pastel hues.

Achillea filipendulina
(ak-i-le'a fil-i-pen-du-li'na)
YARROW

1

Ground cover at its best: ajuga under emerging peonies and lilac.

Ajuga blooming in a shady planting with Japanese painted fern.

Gardeners I know either like ajuga or they don't. When I first started gardening professionally I picked up a prejudice against it from one who didn't. The prejudice lasted until I read *The Education of a Gardener* by Russell Page, and began to understand that almost any plant can be used effectively, whether by design or by culture. My eyes opened further during an English garden tour. There was yucca, of all things, featured in a beautiful planting. I had never liked yucca. I'd always thought of it as ugly and tritely used, which, in the United States, has often been the case. I returned chastened and with a new realization that disliking certain plants had been inhibiting the designing process I had begun. Among other plants, ajuga was now seen in a new light. I began using it regularly when it suited the site I was working on.

'Bronze Beauty', the most prevalent ajuga, is a hard-working perennial. The foliage alone is enough to recommend it, but when it blooms in the spring it bears a profusion of blue-violet blossoms that stand up in whorls on stems about six inches from the foliage. In the close-up photo is a planting of 'Bronze Beauty' with the Japanese painted fern, *Athyrium niponicum* 'Pictum'. The purple blossoms go well with the silver of the fern fronds.

The blossoms of ajuga also look handsome intermingled with spring bulbs, such as tulips and daffodils. Since its foliage is attractive even when it is not in bloom, it is a good ground cover. If you use the cultivar 'Burgundy Glow', even more color can be achieved. The foliage of 'Burgundy Glow' is shiny green with white and pink variegation, so that it makes a colorful planting even by itself.

A. reptans 'Cristata' ('Metallica Crispa' in the trade) has smaller foliage but is tightly crinkled. There is also a showy white-blooming cultivar, 'Alba'.

All the above ajugas are very adaptable to different soil types, and perform like champs in both sun and shade. The plants will spread rapidly into a dense, mat-forming ground cover. In fact, ajuga can become so dense it will choke itself out. This minor flaw can be easily taken care of by occasional thinning.

Because it is so vigorous, ajuga may be able to hold its own under a tree where grass refuses to grow. I like using it at the base of peonies and shrubs, especially 'Burgundy Glow' with blue globosa spruces. Ajuga is an excellent choice for the edge of a perennial garden, along walks, among stepping stones, or, as one friend uses it, in terra cotta pots with yellow-variegated hostas.

ᐏ

Ajuga reptans
(a-ju'ga rep'tanz)
BUGLE

Lady's-mantle foliage.

*Lady's-mantle bloom and leaf texture
harmonize with a white bleeding-heart
and goatsbeard.*

Alchemilla mollis is the best lady's-mantle for our area because it holds up better in the hot summers than others. *A. pubescens* has a bluer, darker leaf, but come summer it burns up more readily and gets terrible spider mites.

A. mollis has unusual chartreuse flowers that look good with the foliage of other perennials. They are arranged in clusters moving up the stalk, resulting in sprays that float above the foliage like dense greenish-yellow clouds. In late spring and early summer, the flowers rise above the plant up to eighteen inches. The stems are long enough to make it an excellent cut flower, especially combined with other yellows and blues. The flowers look terrific in arrangements, and last more than two weeks.

The foliage resembles green umbrellas turned inside out. Individual leaves are widely toothed and covered with fine hairs that trap falling raindrops, so lady's-mantle appears particularly charming during and after a rain. Forming nice mounds, the foliage usually gets up to ten inches, and can spread to twenty-four inches. Best placement is an eastern location to avoid hot midday sun, which encourages spider mites. It can thrive all season in such a situation. If the foliage does turn brown during an extraordinarily scorching summer I usually chop it all off. Lady's-mantle then obliges by putting forth fresh new green foliage.

I've used *A. mollis* in good, rich soil, and have had it do well in worse, such as clay. In both situations the plants had an even supply of moisture. There must be adequate drainage, or else lady's-mantle will rot during our usually wet winters.

Illustrated is a pleasing monochromatic planting of lady's-mantle with a white bleeding-heart, white astilbe, and goatsbeard in the background at left. This part of the garden receives direct eastern (morning) light. Or add more yellow instead for another monochromatic combination that is equally lovely. Plant lady's-mantle with some gold hostas, such as 'Gold Edger', 'August Moon', and the white-edged 'Moonlight'. Lace it all together with *Lysimachia nummularia* 'Aurea', and then stand back and enjoy the warm glow. With either scenario, lady's-mantle adds foliage and flower texture to the grouping.

Lady's-mantle can also be used with contrasting colors. Planted with some blue and white, for example, such as *Geranium* × 'Johnson's Blue' and lamb's-ears, the lady's-mantle looks even richer, and a combination is created that will enhance any garden.

Alchemilla mollis
(al-ke-mill'a mol'lis)
Lady's-mantle

5

*A welcome white in late summer:
Japanese anemone 'Honorine Jobert'.*

*A pink Japanese anemone hybrid, used
as ground cover under trees.*

Japanese anemones bloom from late summer to fall, a time when one has tired of all the hot summer colors. They are easy to mix with other perennials because they come in pink and dark pink as well as white, extending the possibilities of color combinations. A recent Alan Bloom introduction extends the color range even further; a deep rose-magenta semidouble called 'Bressingham Glow', it is recommended by Steven Still in his *Manual of Herbaceous Ornamental Plants,* and should prove to be another jewel once it is widely available in the United States.

The *A. × hybrida* that I've used most is 'Honorine Jobert', a pure white cultivar with abundant flowers. The flowers are two to three inches wide, held on multiple stems, each with a single flower held tight by a fist of dark green sepals, shaped in a perfect sphere. The close-up shows the brilliance of the white petals with the orange-yellow stamens encircling the flower's center. The stems carry the flowers up to four feet above the foliage in a thick mass.

The foliage is a rich dark green and usually stands up to two and one-half feet tall, spreading as wide. The foliage comes up with distinction, covered with dense silver hair. The dark green mass has a good structure before blossoms appear, and remains attractive till the first frost in most of the Lower Midwest. The texture is interesting with other perennials, or standing in a bed all by itself.

A. × hybrida prefers an eastern- or western-facing placement, but I have had it grow successfully in full sun when it can be kept moist. It doesn't like our wet winter soils, but given adequate drainage it should survive. Mulching in northern areas helps to protect over winter, as does avoiding windy situations.

The white blossoms of 'Honorine Jobert' blend nicely with other late summer- and fall-blooming perennials like rudbeckia (as in the closeup), late-blooming phlox, or Russian sage, and with the pink of the hardy begonia blooming at its feet.

Try the Japanese anemone with practically any color combination, and you will soon have a new favorite fall perennial to grace your garden.

Anemone × hybrida
(a-nem'o-nee hib'ri-da)
JAPANESE ANEMONE

The silky sheen of the two-tone 'Robustissima' flowers above the grape-leaf foliage.

Grapeleaf anemone 'Robustissima' blooming in mid-September at Ashland Garden.

Anemone vitifolia 'Robustissima' has been around for a long time, and is my all-time favorite anemone. It grows so vigorously once established that when planted with other perennials it can become invasive; but once you have seen this perennial in bloom, I think you'll agree that it is difficult to have too much. If it does encroach, it is easily removed.

The blossom stalks of *A. v.* 'Robustissima' are shorter than those of *A. × hybrida,* standing at two to three feet, making it a tighter, more compact plant.

The blossom is one of the best pinks ever seen, with two shades of pink underneath serving as the base for a thinly brushed top layer of silver. This combination gives the blossom a silvery sheen that is unusually attractive.

After the flower petals fall, white, woolly seed heads form that provide interest throughout the winter if not removed.

The foliage is a sumptuous green, forming two-foot clumps. As the species name suggests, the leaves do resemble those of grapevines: slightly smaller, but with the same deep lobes and serrated margins. Foliage stays nice-looking most of the season and contrasts well with that of other perennials.

A. vitifolia has proven to be the hardiest anemone I've used, and the one most tolerant of various conditions. It has done equally well for me in full sun and in light shade (meaning it needs bright light—which creates dark hand shadows—all day, or at least four hours' direct morning or afternoon light). This is also the anemone most likely to do best in the upper regions of the Lower Midwest, for it is rated hardy to zone 3. I've sometimes planted it in loamy soil and sometimes in clay that drains well enough, and it has always thrived.

I favor 'Robustissima' because it is shorter and stands up better, at two to three feet, than does the taller *A. × hybrida.* But keep in mind that both are effective however and wherever you use them. 'Robustissima' will also put up with summertime drought.

I like using *A. vitifolia* 'Robustissima' with whites and blues. My favorite combination is with Russian sage for the blue and *Artemisia ×* 'Powis Castle' for the white. To finish off the picture I would use the hulking *Stachys byzantina* 'Helen von Stein', tying all together at the base. Other artemisias would look good with the pink of 'Robustissima' too. I've liked it placed with the blue of Russian sage and the yellow-green of the shrub *Spiraea × bumalda* 'Lime Mound' or 'Goldflame'. It could look great with daisies, or with a background of blue globosa spruce.

☙

Anemone vitifolia
(a-nem'o-nee vit-a-fo'lee-a)
GRAPELEAF ANEMONE

Volunteer columbines, on the right, grace a bed
of peonies and Siberian iris.

Aquilegia canadensis, *our native columbine,
illuminated by morning light.*

10

Once you have columbines you can count on having them for the rest of your life—if not where they were originally planted, then somewhere else in the garden. They definitely travel around by reseeding, but are always delightful in late spring to early summer.

The flowers have long spurs trailing approximately one inch from the petals, looking like octopus tentacles flowing out behind the floating body. There are also five sepals, arranged alternately between the spurs, giving the blossom a balanced stability as if in flight.

Our native *Aquilegia canadensis* has red spurs with yellow sepals, usually hanging with the spurs pointing upward. This position leaves the multiple stamens shooting out the bottom from the flowers' center like fire from the end of a rocket ship. Its space-age appearance is enhanced by the way it floats on top of tall, usually two-foot, stems. Other columbines to try include the 'McKana Hybrids' and the 'Biedermeier' strain, but neither stays around as long as *canadensis*.

Columbine foliage complements the flowers, being grayish-green with a blue cast, two to three lobes, and easy round edges. The plants stand about two feet tall and spread one foot wide. If given a hot exposure in our area the foliage tends to burn up during the summer, but all you have to do to make it look good again is cut it down; fresh foliage will emerge. Leaf miner can be a problem (the insects tunnel through the layers of the leaf, disfiguring it) but, once again, removing and disposing of the infected leaves will keep the insects and the disfiguration to a minimum.

Columbines tend to perform equally well in full sun and half shade, but the flowers last longer in shade. If they don't like where they have been placed, as mentioned earlier, they will go where they get what they want. Good drainage is suggested, but even if the crown dies out during a wet winter, there is the likelihood of new plants from seed. As long as the soil doesn't hold water for more than a couple of hours, columbine should be able to survive.

I've used columbine in both loamy and clay soils. The plants usually last longer in loam, but will put up with poor soil for a couple of years. If you do have to contend with clay soil and don't want to fool with amending it thoroughly, try a top dressing of compost. This will help give the crown a chance to survive. Eventually this top layer will become incorporated into the clay, enriching and improving the texture of the soil.

Columbine can be used with shade-loving plants such as ferns, hostas, and Christmas rose. They all mix nicely, with the columbine adding contrasting color, both with foliage texture and blossom. They are companionable with other perennials, as in the photograph where columbine has self-seeded among a bed of peonies. Columbine works well as a filler here; the same idea could be used with any collection of shrubs.

Aquilegia canadensis
(ak-wi-le'jee-a can-a-den'sis)
WILD COLUMBINE

11

Top center are the three-part leaves of jack-in-the-pulpit, sharing a woodland setting with hostas, bleeding-heart, and an annual red caladium.

A single bloom of jack-in-the-pulpit, showing its distinctive characteristics.

This is a most unusual flowering native. The strange attraction of the flower never diminishes over the years, and its usefulness as a shade plant is difficult to beat. It is called jack-in-the-pulpit because the elongated spathe surrounds and continues upward and over the cylindrical spadix, forming a hood (the pulpit), and the spadix (the jack). The hood is usually four to six inches in height and has a blade that hangs out over the plant. The flower can be light green or purple, striped with a stronger color pattern of the same on the inside.

Arisaema triphyllum usually blooms from early spring to mid-spring in the Lower Midwest. The accompanying close-up, taken on June 6 in central Kentucky, clearly shows the green and white striping pattern of this striking flower.

The foliage offers another attractive aspect of this perennial, being, as its name implies, of three parts. The leaves can be up to nine or ten inches long in three large elliptical lobes held on twelve-inch stems. They cover the flower, and an admirer of jack-in-the-pulpit must consequently either move the leaves aside or bend the knee to look under the foliage. The latter method is the best, and I can think of no better reason to be on one's knees.

I have used *A. triphyllum* in both dappled and half shade and found that the half shade of an eastern-facing situation works just as well as the dappled, woodland setting. The setting photograph reveals *A. triphyllum* in a woodland garden with *Dicentra spectabilis,* hostas, and an annual caladium. The distinctive foliage is just to the left of the dark red caladium with the jack hidden underneath.

Jack-in-the-pulpit will always perform best in a humusy soil that stays moist and drains well—this is, after all, its native habitat. But to stretch the conditions, one can place it in any soil that will drain well with some success. As long as the moisture and the light requirements are available, give it a try. If you do plant it in clay, add some organic matter (pine needles, leaves, etc.), and avoid low-lying areas.

As if the flower and the foliage weren't enough to make this perennial unique, the fall brings another performance treat. The clustered female flowers at the base of the jack are now mature and appear as bright red berries on the stalk of the withered jack. These berries are all the more dramatic because, after the six-month ripening period, they are usually left sticking up all alone above the deteriorated flower and fallen foliage.

A. triphyllum is usually planted with other shade perennials. It is at home with ferns, hostas, and any wildflower, offering a good contrast in foliage texture. Just remember to give them room by not planting companions too closely (a foot to a foot and a half will usually be sufficient). You don't want the foliage of other plants to cover the stalk of bright red berries later in the fall.

Arisaema triphyllum
(a-riss-e'ma tri-fil'lum)
JACK-IN-THE-PULPIT

The cool white foliage of 'Silver King' artemisia with cinnamon fern and columbine.

Artemisia 'Silver Queen' with foxglove, geum, and kniphofia.

14

A very useful native that can eat your garden alive if care is not taken to inhibit it from running everywhere. *Artemisia ludoviciana* 'Silver King' is the one most widely used. The more deeply serrated 'Silver Queen' is also popular. Either can be a problem plant if placed among other perennials because they spread by means of underground stems.

'Silver King' and 'Silver Queen' are mainly grown for their attractive, aromatic foliage, which is a vivid grayish white, and is useful in both fresh and dried flower arrangements. When I plant *A. ludoviciana* I use it as a color blender and to give a cooling effect with green-foliage plants, as in the accompanying photograph. I used artemisia in this location to take advantage of the white foliage in two ways: first to add some relief to all the green of the ferns, and second to tie the planting and the house together.

I don't recommend placing these artemisias with other perennials. I tend to use them in places where they are restricted, or else in clay soil to control their spreading habit. A good example of a restricted place might be between drive and house, or between a walk and a wall, as long as they were not in high-visibility areas. With our summer humidity, artemisias in high-visibility areas can start to look ugly because the foliage tends to deteriorate from the bottom up.

Soil was one factor in choosing the placement of the artemisia in the illustration; it's less rampant in clay. Shade was another. Since artemisias do best in full sun and well-drained soil, I used the lower light situation as part of the controlling strategy. In shade they don't reach the two- to three-foot height they are usually capable of, but do well enough to give the interest and color relief referred to earlier. If you do want to grow the artemisias in full sun and with other perennials, and don't mind pulling out unwanted stems as they invade, they can be used effectively with any pink, lavender, and blue. As mentioned earlier, the white foliage can be used to cool down other greenery, and will have the same effect with hot colors like reds and oranges. The cool white could add some elegance to the cruder rudbeckias, or to those bright annual salvias, either blue or red.

One of the most memorable plantings I've seen using tall artemisias was in England. It was a border featuring vivid red dahlias, blood-red lychnis, and other red-flowering plants. I especially liked one dramatic group of bronze-foliaged red dahlias with a large clump of 'Silver King' artemisia nestling in the middle. The white, red, and bronze were great together.

Artemisia ludoviciana
(ar-te-me'zhe-a lu-do-vis'e-a'na)
WORMWOOD,
WHITE SAGE

The fine texture of 'Powis Castle.'

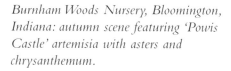

Burnham Woods Nursery, Bloomington, Indiana: autumn scene featuring 'Powis Castle' artemisia with asters and chrysanthemum.

16

Although I haven't used this artemisia very long, I think it is going to be an enormous asset. Tim Morehouse of Cincinnati showed me a plant a few years ago. Impressed with its form, I immediately began using it. I then saw it in the summer of 1994 in a handsome planting in the walled English garden at the Chicago Botanic Garden.

As with most artemisias, the foliage is the main attraction. It resembles a fine-toothed dusty-miller at first glance. It has silvery-white leaves larger than dusty-miller, and a lacier texture than all other artemisias except 'Silver Mound'. The close-up photograph shows the delicate white, filigreed leaves.

Artemisia × 'Powis Castle' gets about three feet tall and spreads to four feet wide, giving it the stature to hold its own with even the largest perennials and shrubs.

'Powis Castle' likes full-sun placement. It forms a neat large mound which makes for an interesting contrast in texture when given all the light it requires. It can tolerate dry situations, and is adaptable to different soils as long as they drain well. Hot, dry summers are certainly to its liking, but I haven't used this perennial long enough to determine how it will stand up to our frequent bouts of humidity.

In the setting photograph, 'Powis Castle' is on the right, planted in front of some taller New England asters, serving to lower the height as the border incorporates shorter perennials in the front of the island bed. The white of this artemisia blends softly with the dark pink and purple asters, creating a neutral backdrop for the yellow chrysanthemum.

I believe this artemisia will prove a valuable asset in today's more easy-going mixed plantings. 'Powis Castle' fits right in with the desire for low-maintenance gardening, standing up and looking good all season.

If there is adequate light, try it out in front of the house to counteract all the green shrubbery. Planted at the center of an island bed with some shorter blue and pink plants surrounding it, 'Powis Castle' would provide structure. Used with the warmer colors of purple salvia and marigolds, it could do the same, and tie the colors together.

Try it with shrubs and perennials, with annuals, or alone by the side door where it will be waiting to greet you like a favorite pet as you enter.

Artemisia ×
'Powis Castle'
(ar-te-me'zhe-a)

The delicate foliage of 'Silver Mound' softens the brick edging.

Bottom, center: even a little splash of silver foliage, from 'Silver Mound' artemisia, brightens the scene.

If any artemisia is truly silver, it is 'Silver Mound'. The soft foliage resembles that of 'Powis Castle', but is finer and more silvery. 'Silver Mound' outshines all the others in the silver department.

The foliage mounds up to about twelve inches, forming precise clumps eighteen inches across. Foliage is so intricate that water droplets are caught between the matted leaves. This beautiful texture can be seen in the accompanying close-up.

A. schmidtiana likes full sun and well-drained, poor soil. Rich soil can cause this artemisia to stretch and open up in the middle. Where do you find poor soil after striving for years to enrich and improve what soil you have? Possibly along the drive, or in ground that hasn't been worked in before. If necessary, go ahead and plant 'Silver Mound' in rich soil; simply cut it back hard before the blossoms open. This takes a little courage but otherwise you will be left with a matted silver mess exactly where you don't want one.

This little beauty is usually used in the front of a planting because of its short stature, and that is the reason I suggest cutting it back to keep it looking good. It is used this way in the setting photograph on the opposite page, seen before it has filled out in June. 'Silver Mound' shares the space with coralbells on the right and candytuft on the left, creating a compatible threesome for the front of this perennial bed. Even though only one-fourth its mature size in the picture, 'Silver Mound' makes an impression as it edges out over the pink-toned brick.

I can't think of a planting that wouldn't be enhanced with 'Silver Mound'. It works overtime contrasting with blues, reds, yellows, and oranges. I tend to prefer it with pinks, blues, and whites. I especially like it in a triangular grouping with some of the shorter hardy geraniums, especially 'Johnson's Blue'. Sometimes the foliage of 'Silver Mound' can rot in our hot and humid summers. If that begins to happen, cut it back to prevent the crown from rotting too. In the northerly regions of the Lower Midwest, this is less likely to be necessary.

Artemisia schmidtiana
'Silver Mound'
(ar-te-me'zhe-a schmit-i-a'na)

Italian arum, in a shady spot with annual impatiens.

The marbled veins of arum leaves.

20

When I was first introduced to this plant, there was nothing to be seen but a stalk sticking up out of the ground with a cluster of orange-red berries clinging to it. I learned that it goes dormant in the heat of summer, to return again in the fall, usually around late September in our area. If the winter is not too severe, it will carry on, providing some welcome greenery in the otherwise bare shade garden. If the foliage does die back, it will make a second appearance in the spring. It is distinctively arrow-shaped, dark green, and marbled with white veins.

The late spring–blooming flowers are similar to those of jack-in-the-pulpit, having a pale green spathe and a spadix (jack) of pale yellow, and just as striking: they look like a tall, slender flame of light green. The arum flower tends to be closer to the ground, and the pulpit does not cover the jack. You have to be quick to see the arum flower, because it stays around for only a few days. As it matures, the foliage begins its decline, leaving the flower more exposed for pollination. Then come the amazing seed pods. After they in turn have disappeared, the foliage makes its reappearance.

Arum italicum 'Pictum' likes to colonize in clumps in partial or full shade. This is a big plus: any plant for full shade is to be appreciated, and this one is particularly showy. It prefers moist, humus-rich soil, but I've had success in lesser soils as long as they drained well. It can encroach on other perennials if not given plenty of space.

I first saw Italian arum planted with other shade-loving plants such as astilbes, ferns, and hostas in one of the nicest gardens in Lexington, that of Harriett Holladay. She had one especially nice composition with snakeroot at the back, glade fern in the middle, and arum in the front. I was to learn much about perennials for shade from this marvelous gardener.

Arum italicum 'Pictum'
(a'rum i-tal'i-cum)
ITALIAN ARUM,
PAINTED ARUM

21

Long fingers of goatsbeard play well in a dark corner.

In the middle of a planting, facing down a holly and providing a background for blue nigella, are the white bloom stalks of goatsbeard.

~

At first glance this American native looks like a very tall astilbe. Further inspection reveals that the goatsbeard leaf is slightly different. The most obvious difference, however, is the much larger size. *A. dioicus* foliage gets up to four feet or more with the flower stalks rising up to six feet. In the accompanying photograph you can see how it towers over its shorter companions. Goatsbeard is a good choice here as a transition plant between heavy, taller shrubs and lighter, shorter perennials.

Another reason to use goatsbeard is that it thrives in partial shade, meaning an east or west location where it can receive up to four to five hours of softer light. I recommend it be kept out of our hot summer sun. It does prefer soil that retains moisture, but some mulch will help here.

Because goatsbeard is so large, spreading up to six feet wide, it is best to decide where it is going to be permanently before planting it. But if you can't decide, don't worry. It would be nice if everything we planted could be placed where it would live for the rest of our days. Goatsbeard gives the gardener a little grace period owing to the fact that it usually takes up to three years to achieve its prominence and stature. It can be moved around for a couple of seasons with no trouble, but might take extra time to reach maturity.

The close-up shows the graceful blossoms. Rising twelve inches above the foliage, they form tall spikes. The photographs here were taken the second week in June, which is when they usually bloom in the Lower Midwest. After the blossoms fade, you can either leave the dried spikes or cut them off.

Even after blossoming the foliage will remain in good condition. This is something to keep in mind when choosing plant materials: you don't have to worry about how to cover a bare space after the plant blooms if the foliage stays attractive. This trait also makes goatsbeard more versatile. It can be used as a transition plant as mentioned above, alone *en masse,* or as a specimen in a highly visible situation. Goatsbeard can even hold the back of a planting, in place of evergreen shrubs.

~

Aruncus dioicus
(a-run'kus di-o'ee-kus)
GOATSBEARD

The bright green foliage of European ginger shines in the morning sun.

European ginger's round leaves create a strong contrast with spring phlox.

The best ginger for perennial gardens is *Asarum europaeum*. Our native ginger, *A. canadense*, has its uses, but the European ginger, although slower-growing and more expensive, stays green and good-looking most of the year. I carried the first European ginger I had ever seen back to Kentucky from Beth Chatto's nursery in England in 1984. She had a thriving colony of it.

A. europaeum has dark, shiny green leaves that remain close to the ground. The shiny foliage catches the light, brightening a shaded area. European ginger would be at home in a woodland garden with dappled shade, perhaps with *Hosta* 'August Moon' behind and *Galium odoratum* in front. You can use this ginger in an eastern-facing placement with equal success.

Being a shade plant, *A. europaeum* likes moisture and a humus-type soil. The garden in the photograph usually gets watered (if it hasn't rained) once a week. This is sufficient to provide the ginger and the other plants with adequate moisture under all but the driest of conditions.

Like the North American ginger, *A. canadense*, the European ginger has a flower that hides next to the ground. This renders the blossom inconsequential as a flowering perennial, but it is worth kneeling down to see. It is bell-like, a blend of purple and brown, sometimes with some green brushed on the outside of the bell.

A. canadense is more heat-tolerant than *A. europaeum*. It can take a drier situation, but even it will need watering if direct sun hits it for more than about three hours a day. If you need a ground cover for an area that is not highly visible, you might try this native ginger. The foliage will deteriorate in late autumn, leaving the area bare, but the plant will not entirely die back. This can be good to hold an otherwise naked area, and if the ginger is planted with other drought-tolerant perennials, its dormancy will go unnoticed.

Asarum europaeum
(as'a-rum u-ro-pe'um)
GINGER

Aster 'Professor Kippenburg' against a lattice fence.

The light purple aster 'Monch' ccomplements the yellow of rudbeckia and the white of Queen Anne's lace.

One of my all-time favorite plants is *Aster × frikartii* 'Monch'. I've seen it bloom here from June till frost in an east location, and its color and height are just what they should be. I didn't think I'd ever use an aster again until about five years ago I tried the 'Monch'.

I had given up on asters because as one progresses as a gardener, one tends to quit growing plants that fall over after the slightest rain unless they are staked and tied. I started with hardy New England asters, *Aster novae-angliae,* taken from Ashland Garden in Lexington, when I was separating an old clump for Louisiana Simpson. Like any novice, I did anything I had to do with a plant to make it look good in my garden. I thought that was what you did. It took years of experience, seeing other gardens, trying other perennials, and most of all listening to other gardeners, to realize that you don't have to put up with unruly plants.

So, over the years I gradually got rid of all my asters because I didn't think there was one that fit my criteria for a good plant: one with a long blooming period that doesn't need special attention to look great, and whose foliage, after blooming, holds its interest for most of the season. I regained my interest in asters, however, when I discovered the 'Monch'.

There is a second-place aster for our area that I must mention, although it tends to flop more than 'Monch'. It is a short New England aster known as *A. novae-angliae* 'Alma Potschke'. (Short for a New England aster means two to three feet tall.) Alma's color is her best characteristic—it's a wonderful bright pink without being garishly bright like electric lipstick. 'Alma Potschke' is a clump-forming aster, and will serve best planted tightly with other perennials for support.

My third favorite aster is *A. novi-belgii* 'Professor Kippenburg'. I've not seen it fall over even a little. It stands about twelve inches tall, and has lavender-blue flowers with a yellow center. The blossoms are smaller than those of 'Monch', but it behaves itself better and is hardier.

The greatest danger to asters is soil that doesn't drain well. In our area this is especially critical. 'Monch' has a tendency to die out during winter because of wet and cold weather, and will need winter protection in the Lower Midwest. According to Steven Still (*Manual of Herbaceous Ornamental Plants),* leaving the stems on the 'Monch' also helps it overwinter. Although the soil must drain well, it doesn't have to be particularly fertile. In hot areas, in fact, asters will tend to do better with infertile soil.

These days I'm less fussy about a little falling over, and I do like these three asters, but there are still better perennials that are easier to use.

Aster
ASTER,
MICHAELMAS DAISY

Astilbe 'Bridesmaid' in a shade garden with a hardy pink geranium to the left and Hosta 'Frances Williams' in the foreground.

'In a wet and sunny location along a front walk, 'Peach Blossom' astilbes steal the scene in mid-June.

The first thing you hear about astilbes is that they are good for the shade. Well, they are. But a beginning gardener doesn't realize that there are different kinds of shade. Astilbes do best in moist shade—ideally half shade, where some light comes through the plants that overhang them, not dark, north-facing, under-the-pine-trees shade. However, even in less than ideal situations they perform well enough. Bright, north-facing light would be satisfactory for astilbes. They can even tolerate hot, direct sun when kept moist. However I have used astilbes, they have never disappointed me.

The Complete Shade Gardener, by George Schenk, has the best definitions of shade. Schenk's term *half shade* is clearer than what seems to be the more prevalent term, *partial shade.* Half shade gives a plant doses of full sun alternating with doses of full shade. An eastern- or western-facing situation will usually yield half shade. Shade perennials, as a general rule, will flourish with three to four hours of this softer light, whereas their foliage will burn in harsh midday sun.

Dappled or filtered shade is probably ideal for most shade perennials. This type of shade is found in a woodland situation, where it is mixed with an equal portion of sun coming through the leaves and branches of taller trees.

If you hold out your hand and can't see a distinct shadow, your shade is probably too dense for most listed shade perennials to thrive. But don't despair; some plants will grow—not necessarily at their best, but well enough to cover an otherwise unsightly area. My advice is to spend time in an area to see exactly how much sun and shade it has—pull up a chair and read a book. Placement decisions are the most important ones a gardener will make.

In a shady or even an eastern-facing position that is moist (it can be an area where water stands for a day or so), astilbes are a fine choice. Keep in mind that if the light is right, moisture can always be added.

Astilbes are adaptable to various types of soil. In the accompanying photograph 'Peach Blossom' astilbes are in front of a house facing northeast. Here they receive about three hours of direct sun in the morning. The subsoil is clay and retains water for extended periods.

Astilbe's flowers are delightfully spiky in a color range from white to deep burgundy-red. Their foliage remains crisp and fernlike after the blossoms fade, and the dried flower stalks can be left on the plant until they are dormant and need cutting back.

Astilbes can be mixed with other shade perennials, such as hostas and ferns, to wonderful effect.

A great, versatile perennial whatever the species and cultivar, astilbe is also a good cut flower. It is best cut when the blossom is half open.

Astilbe
(a-stil'bee)
FALSE SPIREA

The rich bluish-purple blooms of baptisia.

Tall stalks of baptisia behind a bamboo pole (topped with a birdhouse) and 'Johnson's Blue' geranium.

Baptisia australis is a superb plant if you have the space for it. The foliage reaches three and one-half to four feet, while the blossom stalks can reach up to five. With full sun it grows into large, dense clumps that spread about three feet wide. *B. australis* will put up with infertile soils, and even some clay. The specimen illustrated is prospering in some of the finest yellow clay in the Lower Midwest. It does drain well here in this location, and one must keep drainage in mind—not all clay soils will drain quickly enough to allow the planting of certain perennials.

Baptisia is probably the best substitute for lupine in our area. Our summer sun tends to cook lupine foliage and to remind the plant that it is out of place here. Areas in the northern parts of zone 5 might have more success with lupine, but baptisia, being a native, will work throughout the entire Lower Midwest. Baptisia is a very vigorous plant and will last a lifetime once it is settled. It takes two to three years to establish from a gallon container, but it's worth the wait.

From late May to mid-June the tall spikes of false indigo will supply the gardener with rich stalks to cut and use with peonies and other perennials that bloom at the same time. The pea-like blossoms are blue-violet, arranged on handsome gray-green stems, and are seen here with other blue perennials in a sunny border facing southeast. If the blossoms are allowed to remain on the plant they will form black seed pods, excellent for dried arrangements or winter interest. To the left in the photo is an unidentified dark blue Siberian iris. In front of the baptisia is the hardy *Geranium* × 'Johnson's Blue', creating a section of all-blue blossom for early summer.

A fine place for baptisia is the cutting garden. Here it can be on hand for cutting and not impose on other smaller perennials. Or, if you have a situation similar to the one in the illustration, where there is a taller background, such as the brick wall, and a long border, you need look no further. Baptisia is also bold enough to create the background for any planting. Among tall grasses it will give some contrast in texture; standing alone at the corner of a building, it will soften the structure.

Other compatible companions for baptisia would be *Echinacea purpurea* 'Bright Star', *Achillea filipendulina* 'Gold Plate', and *Anemone* × *hybrida,* the Japanese anemone 'Honorine Jobert'. All three can be placed around the baptisia to supply color after it has finished blooming. Thus crowded together, they would not only provide color all season, but help support each other too.

Baptisia australis
(bap-tiz'i-a aus-tra'lis)
FALSE INDIGO

Hardy begonia providing a much-needed
"skirt" for an old barberry.

The pink blossoms and burgundy
stems of hardy begonia glow
in a semi-shady location.

Begonia grandis (formerly *B. evansiana*) is a plant I always think of when someone wants to cover a place in the shade and likes pink. If not planted in the shade around here, the foliage tends to scorch. The foliage shares the same heart-shaped succulence that characterizes some of the tropical houseplant varieties, but it is *hardy*. The buds are a rich pink, and unfold to flowers of a lighter pink with yellow stamens, hanging in clusters from burgundy stems.

Given the shade or soft light they need, you can't ask for a better late summer and fall–blooming perennial. I've placed them in full shade, in an eastern-facing exposure, and given late afternoon light, all with success.

They are also good for a variety of soils, adapting and growing at a rate to satisfy even the most impatient gardener. I've planted them in soils ranging from humus-rich to clay, and not had any problem with them spreading. They do need regular moisture, which means watering once a week in our area, and should not be allowed to dry out completely. In the upper regions of the Lower Midwest a layer of mulch should be applied during the winter months so that the tubers don't freeze.

I think they are best planted by themselves or under shrubs and trees, rather than with other perennials. When planted with other perennials they can be invasive. We maintain one garden that is over sixty years old in which the begonia is so well established that we have to pull it up in vast amounts weekly when it starts to appear. But one can take advantage of this prolific tendency, using it as suggested.

In the accompanying photograph, *B. grandis* has established itself into a "skirt" around an ancient shrub of barberry. This was quite unintentional, but when the first seedling came up it was left to grow. Volunteers were welcome in this situation: the old barberry branches no longer covered the scruffy base, leaving an unsightly patch of weeds underneath. The begonias have grown to smother all the weeds and dress the base in a most pleasing fashion.

A surprise awaits anyone who first looks through a hardy begonia plant with the sun hitting it just right. There is a glow of red on the underside of the leaves, a luminous grainy burgundy that sparkles, which, once witnessed, is never forgotten. But you must bend down to observe this phenomenon, or cut them and take them inside to enjoy in a flower arrangement. They make a delightful cut flower; even after the pink petals drop, the ripened ovaries continue to give color as they hang on the stems.

Begonia grandis self-sows readily. It will surprise you from year to year by popping up everywhere, but it is such a treasure that you won't mind.

Begonia grandis
(be-go'ni-a gran'dis)
HARDY BEGONIA

To the right of the Japanese silver grass in this street planting stands the boltonia, just beginning to show its white blossoms.

34

Somewhat resembling a tall white aster, *Boltonia asteroides* 'Snowbank' is another fall-blooming perennial. The flowers are white with yellow centers, approximately one inch wide, and daisylike. The profuse blossoms can be seen in the close-up photograph, atop sturdy four- to five-foot-tall stems. In the setting photograph the white boltonia is on the far right with taller grasses in the rear and faced down with the yellow of *Rudbeckia fulgida* 'Goldsturm' and the pink and russet of *Sedum* 'Autumn Joy'.

Boltonia is used to good effect in this scene, its foliage breaking the monotony of the grasses. It is conspicuous enough to hold its own with other bold perennials, as in the photograph, or to serve as the anchor for a planting of smaller perennials. It doesn't bloom long, but its white flowers are welcome at this time of year. Boltonia is native to the eastern U.S.

The cultivar 'Snowbank' seems to be the most favored because, if grown in the full sun it does best in, it doesn't need any staking or support. However, there is another boltonia called 'Pink Beauty', of shorter stature, only three to four feet in height. I've seen this one only in gallon pots, but it is a good medium pink with the same yellow center as 'Snowbank'. Both are rated hardy to zone 4.

> ☙
>
> *Boltonia asteroides*
> (bol-to'ne-a as-ter-oy'des)
> WHITE BOLTONIA

A good white for September:
'Snowbank' boltonia.

The dainty blossom clusters of brunnera.

The cool blue of brunnera in dappled light with spring violets and white spring beauties.

This is my favorite plant to use with daffodils and tulips in the spring. Its bright blue forget-me-not-like flowers enrich all the fresh yellows and other colors of spring. Brunnera's blue flowers stand above the heart-shaped, dark green foliage in loose sprays approximately eighteen inches tall, darker than the annual forget-me-not, with a pale yellow eye. They are impressively showy even though they are only one-quarter inch wide.

It gets its species name from the size of the leaves, up to eight inches across. Although belonging to the borage family, brunnera has a softer look which redeems it. The hairy leaves emerge a bright green in the spring, enlarging and darkening as they mature. Fresh green leaves appear all season. Individual plants usually stand about one foot tall and spread up to eighteen inches wide, forming nice round clumps. The foliage remains attractive throughout the season, adding a pleasing shape and texture to any planting and making this plant a good ground cover.

This little wonder does best in partial shade—three to four hours of direct light—but I have used it with some success in full sun if there is plenty of moisture. An eastern- or western-facing position is the best in a direct sun situation. The blooms last approximately two months, a fairly long time for a perennial.

Brunnera flourishes in well-drained, humus-rich, moist soil. If you have a bare area under a tree where you have tried growing grass for a decade and it gets the required light and moisture, then try brunnera. It is vigorous, and spreads by reseeding itself. Once you garden with this plant you soon discover that it is difficult to get too much. If it does reseed itself where it's not wanted, it is easy to control.

By looking ahead when designing, one can make use of brunnera's robust spreading habit to grow old with. All of us sooner or later find that we must slow down in the garden; we can't take care of as many acres as we used to. Left alone, brunnera will eventually take over. If we allow brunnera to do what it does naturally—dominate—we'll have less to do ourselves. What could be a better fate than a wealth of brunnera blooming all over the place?

Brunnera is exceptional planted with hostas because it blooms and fills in while the hostas are coming up. A planting like this which I did in 1983 is still thriving. Brunnera will serve the same purpose with ferns, the large leaves creating a good contrast to the upright fern fronds.

Whether you use this perennial with other plants or by itself, it is difficult to find a better-performing plant.

Brunnera macrophylla
(brun-ne'ra mak-ro-fil'a)
SIBERIAN BUGLOSS,
SUMMER FORGET-ME-NOT

'White Clips' on the right, in a bed with astilbes and fringed bleeding-heart in the back.

Campanula 'White Clips'.

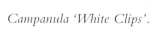

The campanula family has many uses, from ground cover to cut flower. Campanulas come in sizes ranging from six inches to three feet, and bloom from June till October; adding to their value, most of them are blue. One of the smallest is the Carpathian bellflower, *Campanula carpatica* 'Blue Clips'. It appears more of a lilac-blue than a true blue. Botanically the coloration is caused by the presence of the blue pigment anthocyanin in the flower cells. This is why you will encounter purple flowers that are described as blue. The blue is there, mixing with red, and visually appearing purple.

There are also white forms of *C. carpatica,* the most widely used being 'White Clips'. The accompanying close-up photograph shows 'White Clips' in late July, its flowers, shaped like little two-inch bells, positioned erect on the stems. 'Blue Clips' and 'White Clips' bloom from early to midsummer, sometimes sending up flowers into late summer.

Both 'Blue Clips' and 'White Clips' have the same tidy leaves—like elongated, crinkled-edged hearts—with a light green texture. The foliage grows up to six inches tall, forming neat mounds that eventually increase and spread into large clumps, making it a good choice for the front of a planting.

Carpathian bellflowers do nicely in anything from full sun to partial shade. I have found that they prefer eastern, morning light, when the sun is not too hot. They usually put on a burst of growth in the spring, then slow down in our hot, humid summers. Either very dry or very wet soils retard their growth; and if kept too wet during the winter, they rot easily. But if given sufficient sun, the well-drained soil they like, and constant moisture, they should thrive. A porous mulch of small pine bark nuggets or pine needles over the root area will protect them from rotting during the winter. Take care not to smother the crown: never place the mulch directly on top of the plant.

These plants are too small for other use than in the front of a planting, or massed by themselves. I use them on the edge of larger plantings, in groups of at least three, depending on the length and depth of the planting. The longer and wider it is, the larger the clump needs to be to make a good showing. They are also effective between stepping stones, planted alone in planters or urns, or in one of those rock gardens so common in the horticultural literature and so rare in real life.

In the other photograph, *C. carpatica* 'White Clips' is shown with companions, *Astilbe × arendsii* 'Fanal' and the fringed bleeding-heart, *Dicentra eximia* 'Bountiful'. They form a compatible grouping both culturally and for textural interest.

Campanula carpatica
(cam-pan'u-la kar-pat'i-ka)
CARPATHIAN
BELLFLOWER

Blue and white peach-leaved bellflowers
in a bright location with daisies and
pink spirea.

Peach-leaved bellflower is tall enough to use
for cutting. The blue variety is seen here
with coreopsis.

This bellflower is tall enough to make a good cut flower as well as a delightful perennial for the garden. *C. p.* 'Grandiflora Alba' is a popular white variety, having two-inch-wide flowers. 'Telham Beauty' grows four feet tall and offers rich blue blossoms two to three inches across.

The blossoms face outward from the stem. Their shape is like those of the preceding bellflower, only larger. Because of their size, they are showier in a border, especially when planted *en masse* for effect. The flowers appear in late spring or early summer, and plants will continue into July if the old blossoms are removed. The leaves are long and slender, reaching eight inches, with rounded teeth. Stems reach two to three feet tall, with an eighteen-inch span.

Peach-leaved bellflower grows well in sun or the half shade of an eastern-facing placement. Well-drained soil is required, but not high fertility, so it is fairly versatile for use in the landscape.

Plants of either the blue or the white bellflower are best placed in large groups (seven or more) for better display and to give improved support for their long stems. All peach-leaved bellflowers look good with daisies, coreopsis, and *Malva alcea* 'Fastigiata'. When they are going to be used for cutting, I usually plant two dozen. This allows plenty for that purpose while leaving some to maintain color among other perennials.

Peach-leaved bellflower can be used in the middle of a planting or at the front. They naturalize readily if the situation is suitable, and, because of their height, are very effective among wildflowers.

The only problem I have encountered with *C. persicifolia* is slugs. A layer of sand around the base of the plant will discourage them.

Campanula persicifolia
(cam-pan'u-la per-sik-i-fo'lee-a)
PEACH-LEAVED
BELLFLOWER

The shining stars of Serbian bellflower at home with lamb's-ears.

Serbian bellflower with hosta, annual begonias, and, top left, the spectacular white blooms of strawberry geranium (Saxifraga stolonifera), usually grown as a houseplant, which is hardy in this Zone 6 garden.

This campanula is lower and more spreading than *C. carpatica.* The blooms are smaller, and the plant has different uses. Its half-inch, star-shaped flowers, light purple with white centers, make up for their small size by literally covering the mound of foliage in early summer. If the summer happens to be cooler than average, this perennial will continue to bloom intermittently. Usually, blossoms begin in early May in the Lower Midwest, and continue into July.

In the close-up photograph of Serbian bellflower you can see the abundant upward-facing blossoms and the small heart-shaped leaves, sharing the edge of a perennial garden with the soft white foliage of lamb's-ears. Each leaf is about one-half inch wide and long, on a longer stem which allows the foliage to mash down after a rain, then make a satisfactory recovery afterwards.

Although *poscharskyana* remains the best campanula for Lower Midwest gardens, *C. carpatica* 'Blue Clips' and 'White Clips' are the two found most often in the trade because these are the larger-flowering hybrids. I feel *C. poscharskyana* should be carried by more nurseries. Not only are its flowers more profuse, but the plant is more reliable in our wet and cold winters. The constant freezing and thawing takes its toll on other campanulas.

Of all their requirements, well-drained soil is the most important, not only for winter survival but for their general culture. One note of caution is useful here: don't leave campanulas covered too long after winter if they have been mulched. They can rot easily with a mulch holding moisture against their fleshy crowns.

The Serbian bellflower is quite versatile in its range of light requirements, thriving in full sun to half shade. I've used it both on the edge of woodland gardens, where it gets only three hours of direct morning sun, and in south-facing positions with success.

As this perennial spreads, it forms round mounds from the center outward. After two or three years the crown of the plant usually becomes bare in the middle. At this point the plant has usually grown sufficiently that all that is necessary is to dig up a small section of the new growth and replant it back to the center.

Serbian bellflowers are so short that they need to be at the front of a planting if used with taller perennials. In a border I usually begin by planting three together because it takes that many to make an impression. In half shade they can be planted with hostas, ferns, geraniums, or any other shade-loving perennial to introduce a height change for contrast. They are also small enough to be used in pots, and can be tucked in between stepping stones as long as they are kept moist and not walked on continuously.

Campanula
poscharskyana
(cam-pan'u-la po-shar-skee-ah'na)
SERBIAN BELLFLOWER

*A blue and white combination using plumbago
and hydrangea.*

*Plumbago (leadwort) offers one of the best
blues for the garden.*

Its flower color is this plant's most unique characteristic. The blossoms are a cobalt blue, deep, like dark delphinium blue. Up close you can see the purple there, but from a distance this underused perennial washes the scene with deep blue. The flowers are borne in tight clusters, interesting in themselves for their pincushion shape and russet coloration, about one-half inch in width, carried on a long neck, or corolla, like phlox. This detail can be seen in the accompanying close-up photograph.

The blue is good planted under shrubs to ground and accentuate the larger mass. In the setting photograph, blue plumbago has been planted alongside *Hydrangea paniculata* 'Grandiflora' at a house corner facing east that gets southern sun too. Both photos were taken in early September; the plumbago had been blooming since late August and would continue until late fall.

Fall brings another treat from blue plumbago as the foliage turns from green to reddish brown. The leaf shape is interesting —an elongated diamond. Plant height is from eight to twelve inches, and spread is up to eighteen inches. Older plantings tend to intertwine, forming a dense mat that will crowd out weeds.

Both flowers and foliage make this an excellent plant for late summer and fall color. *Ceratostigma plumbaginoides* is at home when grown in either half shade or full sun. It does tend to stay shorter when grown in partial shade, but shines all the brighter without the sun washing out the color.

Plumbago likes well-drained soil; it will rot in soggy conditions. I've used it in different soil types with some success, and even had some establish itself in mild clay. As long as the soil drains well and the light is right, give it a try. The one temptation to stay away from is planting it under trees: tree roots give too much competition.

Try plumbago's intense blue to add fall color to any shrub planting. In the foreground of the usual foundation planting, it can enhance any color of brick and tie the shrubs and house to the lawn in a soothing way. Or use it with black-eyed Susans to complement the yellow. One of my favorite ways to use plumbago is with white-foliaged plants such as lamb's-ears or artemisia; the deep blue flowers and, later, the red foliage with the silver of the other plants make a wonderful combination for any garden. Used as a ground cover, in addition to providing color, leadwort will tie a planting together.

Ceratostigma plumbaginoides
(ser-at-o-stig'ma plum-ba'ji-noi'deez)
BLUE PLUMBAGO,
LEADWORT

'Single Apricot' sharing a cut-flower garden
with annual blue salvia and lavender
on the right.

Chrysanthemum 'Single Apricot'.

46

Everyone is familiar with the plant called *Chrysanthemum × morifolium*—the garden mum—with its bright cushions of flower heads in the fall. It has an established place in American gardens. (Recently the taxonomists have been busy with all the chrysanthemums, scattering some to other genera. The garden mum's scientific name, for example, has been changed to *Dendranthema × morifolium*. Not to worry, though, most catalogs continue to use the old names, so there's no difficulty locating them.)

But there are other fall chrysanthemums that also have value and deserve wider use. 'Single Apricot' is one of them. It usually can be found listed in the trade as *Chrysanthemum* 'Single Apricot' Korean. It is of unknown parentage, but one of its ancestors may well have been *Chrysanthemum coreanum,* the Korean daisy, a single white, hardy chrysanthemum that blooms very late.

I first saw this beautiful mum on a late-September tour of Burnham Woods Nursery in Bloomington, Indiana. Its single apricot blossoms quickly caught my attention as we walked through the gardens. The plants I brought home bloomed in October, when the accompanying photographs were taken. The flowers are a rich apricot when they first open, with the usual yellow center of mums, fading to a lighter tint as they mature. It is the best apricot color I've seen in a chrysanthemum. Foliage is a typical dark green, borne on almost black stems. The plant gets close to eighteen inches tall and spreads approximately two feet wide.

Light and soil requirements are the same for *C.* × 'Single Apricot' as for *C.* × *morifolium,* drainage being critical for Lower Midwest winter survival. Otherwise, it is extremely hardy. Pinching is unnecessary.

The color of this outstanding mum is wonderful with the silvery-white foliage of lavender 'Hidcote', seen to the right of 'Single Apricot' in the setting photograph. Purple shades of annual salvia and petunia are softened by the pastel apricot, a subtle alternative to the stronger tones of the more common garden mum.

Chrysanthemum ×
'Single Apricot'
(kris-anth'e-mum)

A garden chrysanthemum at the base of yellow
and orange zinnias.

The brassy fall-blooming chrysanthemum
'Dark Triumph'.

48

These are the perennials that announce fall in the garden; but I have found they live up to their reputation for hardiness better if planted in the spring. Then again, if we have one of our wet and cold Midwest winters, they can rot or freeze out no matter when they are planted. But spring planting immensely increases their chance of survival.

There is no perennial more used in the fall to provide instant color. Nothing wrong with this, if you keep in mind that planting mums in the fall is using them as an annual. The flowers come in a range from white to bronze, with lavender, yellow, red, and orange in between; if the plant has been pinched back until August, it will usually be a solid mass of color in September.

Pinching the buds off until August is important: the chrysanthemums will finish blooming before autumn even begins if the buds are left to develop without intervention. Since I have vast quantities of chrysanthemums to control, I usually go over the entire heads of plants with clippers instead of pinching each bud off individually. To avoid that evenly sheared, domelike look, I try to clip unevenly, making them appear more natural.

The foliage is dark green and deeply toothed, forming one- to three-foot mounds. The plants usually spread as wide as they are tall, creating a substantial presence in groups of three or more. (Another advantage of spring planting is that the chrysanthemums then have time to grow into their natural shapes, allowing their structure to add texture and form to the garden.) Because of their size at maturity, chrysanthemums can hold positions from the middle of a perennial grouping to the front of a border. They can also be massed together for vast displays of color.

Chrysanthemums need to be in full sun to do their best. Another requirement is moist, well-drained soil. They will benefit from supplemental water applied in the heat of our Lower Midwest summers. Well-drained soil is particularly helpful during our wet winters, this being the most likely time for the mums to rot. A monthly feeding is also worth the effort.

Because chrysanthemums come in such a wide range of colors, they can be used just about anywhere. More colors come out seemingly every year, including softer, muted tones like pink and buff, which are easier to blend with other perennials. Try some of the many cultivars offered by White Flower Farm, such as the pastel orange 'Best Regards', the buff-pink 'Whip-poor-will', and the blood-red 'Vampire', or try the spring-offered selections at your local nursery.

Chrysanthemum ×
morifolium
(Dendranthema × morifolium)
(kris-anth'e-mum mor-i-fol'i-um)
GARDEN MUM

The Nippon daisy blooms in October.

The white of Nippon daisy in a fall border at Burnham Woods Nursery, Bloomington, Indiana.

The flower of this Japanese native resembles that of the wild ox-eye daisy so common in the Lower Midwest. Usually about three inches in diameter, it has the typical white petals radiating around a yellow center. The surprising thing about it is its very late bloom period—October in Cincinnati, where I first saw it a few years ago. After the initial shock, it was quite a treat to see daisies in the fall. Like the garden chrysanthemum, this one has been reclassified. Look for *Nipponanthemum nipponicum* if you can't find it under the name given above. It is rated hardy to zone 5.

To see these flowers in the late fall is like spring revisited. They seem out of place until you get used to the idea of having daisies around from mid to late fall (how difficult can that be?). *Chrysanthemum nipponicum* is at a definite advantage in being a white late-bloomer among the sea of autumn colors.

Its disadvantage is the possibility that an early frost may freeze the blossoms. But don't let that stop you from taking a chance on this daisy; it is worth having around for those times when we don't get an early frost.

At first I had poor success with the Nippon daisy; I was trying to use it in soil that didn't drain well enough. Once I moved it to a sunny spot with better drainage it was fine. In our area, provided it has good drainage, *C. nipponicum* can tolerate a variety of different soil textures.

Thanks to its flowering characteristics, it supplies a much-needed color with which to design during the fall. White at that time of year can be used to advantage by placing it among or in groupings next to the brighter autumn colors to soften or contrast. I tend to use it in plantings with earlier-blooming perennials, such as Siberian iris and lavender, to make a show later in the season.

The foliage of *C. nipponicum* looks nothing at all like that of our wild daisy. It is attractive even before the plant blooms—dark green, thick, and succulent—and tends to mound up like a shrub. It is supposed to reach three feet in height but I haven't seen it over one and a half feet tall in our area. Although Nippon daisy is inclined to act like a shrub and lose foliage at the bottom when it does reach its full height, that can easily be dealt with by planting shorter perennials around it.

ᘒ

Chrysanthemum
nipponicum

(kris-anth'e-mum nip-pon'i-kum)

NIPPON DAISY

The miniature daisy, feverfew.

Feverfew blends with the white stripes of Japanese silver grass in the background, contrasting in texture with the dried seed heads of nigella.

Here's a perennial that returns mostly by reseeding itself. *Chrysanthemum parthenium* does come back from the crown but in addition pops up in other parts of the garden on its own. It makes an excellent filler among other plants, and is easily controlled if not wanted.

The flowers, in the form of a miniature daisy, are small, but they appear in dense clusters on stems twenty-four to thirty-six inches tall, making an impressive display from midsummer to fall.

Beneath the tightly clustered blossoms lies ferny foliage that is pungently aromatic when it is brushed against. Leaves are a grayish-green, deeply lobed and serrated, which gives the foliage its ferny quality. The texture of the foliage complements that of daylilies and rudbeckia. Individual plants of feverfew can spread two feet or more, adding color and form to any planting.

C. parthenium does best with a sunny exposure, but I have seen it escape to shadier areas and bloom. Four hours of direct light seems to be the minimum required; the plant tends to be weaker and fall over in the shade. I've had it do well in a variety of soil types, even clay, as long as drainage was satisfactory.

Feverfew is effective planted with just about any other perennial requiring sun most of the day. Both foliage and flowers will provide contrast and texture in most perennial groupings. I like to plant feverfew all over the yard to help tie everything together, and have begun using it in cutting gardens, as it makes a fine cut flower. In bloom it is a good filler in bouquets. Even when it isn't blooming, the foliage is nice in a vase with roses.

I fill in with *C. parthenium* among daylily plantings, in front of peonies, around leggy perennials, and at the base of shrubs. It is ideal to start a new perennial border with because it can take up space while slower-growing plants are maturing. As the other perennials come to size, excess feverfew is easily yanked out to make room.

Chrysanthemum parthenium
(kris-anth'e-mum par-thee'ne-um)
FEVERFEW

The popular daisy 'Mt. Shasta'.

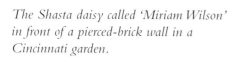

The Shasta daisy called 'Miriam Wilson' in front of a pierced-brick wall in a Cincinnati garden.

54

The Shasta daisy, with its three-inch white rays around a yellow center, is one of the all-time favorites. You'll want to try them all after looking in a catalog and seeing the many cultivars. They come in large singles, lacy doubles, small semi-doubles. Flowers can be had up to seven inches across with the cultivar 'Polaris'; if large is what you want, this is the one. Most cultivars are listed as hardy to zone 5. This is not always how it works out in reality; I suggest that *Chrysanthemum × superbum* 'Alaska' (hardy to zone 4) be used in the upper regions of the Lower Midwest. If you keep the old flowers deadheaded, your Shastas may be encouraged to bloom until frost. As cut flowers, they are excellent and long lasting in arrangements.

The dark green leaves are several inches long, and serrated like an oblong saw. Most plants will reach up to two feet wide, the smaller cultivars like 'Little Miss Muffet' making tidy round mounds.

Shasta daisies need full-sun exposure to do well: not necessarily full all day, but at least six hours of direct light. The foliage can wilt on our hot summer days, but if kept moist the plant usually perks back up when the sun moves away. Fertile soil is another requirement for daisies. But probably the most important need for *C. × superbum* is good drainage. This is critical during our wet winters because the crowns will rot if they are held in water for days at a time.

C. × superbum is most dramatic against a dark background of other green foliage. The white blossoms of 'Mt. Shasta' glow in the accompanying close-up, seen here with a taller background of green foxglove foliage. With contrasting companions—foxgloves, a spot of yellow coreopsis in the background, coralbells and 'Silver Mound' artemisia in the front—it makes an attractive planting in June.

Since Shasta daisies come in a variety of heights, they can be used in different parts of any sunny planting. Taller cultivars can be placed in the rear of a border, in the middle, or serve as the background perennial placed in front of shrubs, fences, and walls. Shorter cultivars tend to work better from the middle to the front of a grouping.

However you choose to use them, remember to divide Shasta daisies every other year or so to increase their vigor.

Chrysanthemum ×
superbum
(Leucanthemum × superbum)
(kris-anth'e-mum su-per'bum)
SHASTA DAISY

A great white clematis, 'Huldine'.

'Huldine' with thalictrum, rose, and lily, anchored with lamb's-ears, in a Cincinnati garden.

It is my intention to write here of a clematis other than the more common ones sold—not that they aren't worthy in the garden, but that there are so many other excellent ones. You need look no further than the Wayside or Park's catalogs to find the large, colorful pinwheels with names like *Clematis* × *jackmanii* and *C.* 'Henrii'. They are deservedly famous and readily available, and have paved the way for the larger selection of not-so-well-known ones that have recently appeared on the market, among them *Clematis* 'Huldine', one of the more vigorous I have used. Vigor is the key. If you have found it difficult to get other clematis started, try this one.

'Huldine' is a white late bloomer, not as big as some of the better known, earlier-blooming clematis, but striking in June. Six petals of brilliant whiteness open to reveal pale yellow stamens that later turn a darker yellow, and have a mauve tinge at maturity. The blossoms fold out to about four inches across, and will linger for about two months. The foliage remains attractive for most of the growing season. It is the typical three-part leaf, and is carried on dark reddish-brown stems.

The depicted specimen of *C.* 'Huldine' is facing southwest, with other perennials planted in front of it to keep the root area cool. An east-facing location would be good for 'Huldine' too, one with four hours' direct light but no hot midday sun. If you must place a clematis in full sun, be sure to keep the roots cool and give it even moisture.

If kept either too dry or too wet, the plant may brown out early or succumb to the infamous clematis wilt. Soil with a high organic content helps retain the needed moisture. It is best not to mulch clematis heavily in our Lower Midwest summers; that promotes clematis wilt also. Instead, grow shallow-rooted perennials or annuals in front to keep the root area cool. I have had success with keeping the roots cool, when starting clematis, by placing large, flat stones over the root area, thus shading and retaining moisture.

My favorite medium for supporting climbers such as clematis or climbing roses is copper wire, mounted on wood, stone, or brick with copper (or easier-to-find brass) screw eyes and molly bolts. The method is fully explained and illustrated in *Basic Projects and Plantings for the Garden* (1993), published by Stackpole Press.

Clematis are usually grown on walls, but they have other uses. As Christopher Lloyd so succinctly puts it, clematis are fine companions for climbing roses, "each attempting to bury its defects in the other's embrace." A clematis grown with shrubs and permitted to run over and through them adds an unexpected spot of color to their drab greenness. Clematis is an outstanding asset in any mixed shrub and perennial border, bringing color and texture, and can be a welcome sight climbing through a tree.

Clematis 'Huldine'

(klem'a-tis hool-deen')

The intense purple flowers of
tube clematis.

Tube clematis alongside a short, early
daylily, shown to convey an idea
of its habit and size.

60

I first purchased this plant for a client who collects perennials, thinking of it as a curiosity and nothing more. It was sitting in a Cincinnati nursery, labeled "shrub clematis," and being a deprived Kentucky gardener seeing that it was something different, I bought it immediately.

But *Clematis heracleifolia* has turned out to be much more than a curiosity. It is an unusual treasure that begins blooming in June in the southern part of the Lower Midwest. Its small flowers need close attention to be appreciated, but are well worth the effort. Blossoms are inch-long, purple and white striped tubes, with four darker purple sepals peeled back to reveal a bright yellow center. The flowers develop in clusters at the end of the stems, and gather in whorls all along the elongated branches where the leaves are attached. They look like miniature hyacinths, blooming through August. Afterward come the fluffy seed heads.

Since the foliage is ungainly, reaching up to four and one-half feet tall on weak branches, it is advisable to plant tube clematis with support nearby. The house wall not only helps to support the branches, but makes a nice backdrop for displaying the structure of the plant.

This tube clematis is facing east, receiving about three hours of direct sunlight in the morning. It has done well here but would be good in full sun too, surrounded by other perennials. More sun would help strengthen the stems, and the other perennials would provide some support.

Another suitable place for this shrub clematis would be along a walk or at the end of a path where passers-by can appreciate the small blossoms. I think some sort of background is advisable when planting this clematis, because it is such a sparsely branched plant.

Soil requirements are the same as for other clematis: organic matter and even moisture. The soil need not be perfect. The clematis in the photographs is planted in yellow clay that has had organic matter dug in at planting time.

Any way you choose to use this unusual perennial, it is sure to be a conversation piece in your garden.

*Autumn clematis climbing up the side
of an arbor.*

*Sweet autumn clematis cascading over
a wrought-iron fence.*

62

Probably the most vigorous of all clematis, *Clematis paniculata* has a profusion of sweetly scented creamy-white blossoms in late summer. It is one of the best for the Lower Midwest. This clematis has escaped cultivation and can sometimes be seen along roadsides throughout rural areas, especially in the south. It is common and ordinary, but so effective—if used with a little imagination.

The individual flowers are only about an inch wide but come on such a huge mass of foliage that they can cover an area up to thirty feet wide. After about three weeks, the blossoms fade and fuzzy seed heads appear, adding another attraction. Since these seeds are dispersed throughout a wide area, new seedlings often pop up where least expected. Obtaining a start from someone who grows this clematis is not difficult.

On a mature plant, I have seen the foliage grow nearly thirty feet after it has been cut all the way down to the ground. The leaves themselves act as tendrils, grabbing onto anything available, growing upward and outward. Leaves are in three parts and dark green, remaining fresh looking until the blossoms cover them up.

C. paniculata prefers full, direct sun all day, yet I have seen it doing fine in the shade. Soil must drain well, but autumn clematis is adaptable to less than ideal soil types, although clay might slow it down a bit. Within three years, under a variety of conditions, this vigorous clematis can reach maturity. It does not hesitate to cover arbors, trellises, fences, and walls. Given something to clamber on, it can hide any unsightly outdoor structure. Use it near a doorway and breathe in its sweet scent as you enter the house. Or let it climb up through that old yew out front to cover the top, like icing on a cake.

Whatever you do, take time to cut some and bring it inside. The blossoms don't last long in water, but they will scent an entire room.

> ᥫᩤ
>
> *Clematis paniculata*
> *(C. maximowicziana)*
>
> (klem'a-tis pan-i'cu-lah'ta)
>
> AUTUMN CLEMATIS,
> VIRGIN'S BOWER

A complementary combination: rich yellow coreopsis 'Nana' with the blue of annual nigella and the lighter yellow of moneywort.

The soft yellow coreopsis 'Moonbeam' with coralbells, lily, and foxgloves.

I quit using most tall coreopsis years ago. With their large, heavy blossoms on weak, thin stems, they either fell over or required staking. Staking is not necessarily a bad word if you like a plant well enough to go to the trouble, but it is undeniably more work than some of us want to do—especially when there are other plants that will perform without assistance. Thus, evolution led me to shorter coreopsis. Weak-stemmed cultivars can always be controlled if planted with supportive companions, but on the whole I find the shorter ones more serviceable. All the tickseeds, incidentally, are native to North America.

Coreopsis tend to be yellow—various shades of golden yellow, running to yellow-orange—with one pink, the one- to three-foot *Coreopsis rosea*. Flowers range from one to two inches wide, with multiple petals forming daisy-like rays around the yellow centers. Bloom begins in mid-spring with the six- to nine-inch *C. auriculata* 'Nana' and continues all through summer with the two- to three-foot *C. grandiflora* 'Early Sunrise', a semi-double, if the old flowers are regularly removed.

Among the taller ones are several that are controllable. One is the three-foot *C. verticillata* 'Golden Showers'. The finely textured foliage evidently laces the stalks together to form a self-supporting plant. Another, *C. v.* 'Moonbeam', is an excellent soft, buttery-yellow. Although it is one of the taller ones, 'Moonbeam' is self-supporting. It blends subtly with other perennials and blooms for a very long time. Its finely woven foliage makes neat, round mounds, which the flowers blanket in a dense cover.

The foliage offered by coreopsis varies. All except the verticillatas have long, medium to dark green, lance- or oblong-shaped leaves. The verticillatas have a fine-textured leaf, separated into three threadlike filaments.

I've tried the above-mentioned coreopsis in soils that ranged from clay to humus-rich, and obtained the best results in the lesser soils as long as there was good drainage. A better plant for sunny spots where the soil is lacking nutrients is difficult to come by.

All coreopsis grow their best in full sun. Most prefer hot and dry situations; they actually do better in dry sites, except for *C. a.* 'Nana', which likes to be kept moist. The verticillatas are especially dependable for hot and dry areas. Use them all to advantage with purple perennials such as foxglove, geraniums—especially 'Johnson's Blue'—and coralbells, and with annuals like nigella (love-in-a-mist), which is one of the best blues in all of horticulture. Add some *Artemisia* 'Powis Castle' or lamb's-ears for an outstanding combination.

Coreopsis
(kor-e-op'sis)
TICKSEED

A close look at the lacy blossom heads of Queen Anne's lace.

Queen Anne's lace behind the white lily 'Casa Blanca'. Both are wonderful for cutting.

Most reference works call this wildflower of European origin an unsuitable garden plant. But if its less desirable characteristics are kept in check, Queen Anne's lace can be tamed with fine results. Moreover, if you dislike using toxic chemicals to control insect pests, an excellent alternative is to garden with plants that attract the "good bugs"—predators—to your yard. Queen Anne's lace is one of the finest for this purpose. It also acts as a host for the larvae of Black Swallowtail butterflies.

Queen Anne's lace is unrivaled as a cut flower; there is no other that can match its lacy white delicacy. Each bloom measures up to eight inches across on a stem that rises four feet tall or more. The tiny white flowers that make up the round, flat clusters bloom through July and August, and usually well beyond. The compound and fernlike foliage, as delicate as the blossoms, increases its aesthetic value. The leaves are dark green, a good complement to the flowers.

Full sun is a necessity for Queen Anne's lace. It will stand up to four feet tall in the least of soils, and can be used to advantage in clay. In fact, *D. carota* thrives on infertile ground, and can be found naturalized in hot and dry conditions. You can see it all over America in fields and along roadsides.

It is in reality a rampant biennial that acts like a perennial. The gardener does have to take some precautions with it, but given a place out of the main garden it will prove extremely useful. And even in a garden setting, Queen Anne's lace can be controlled by weeding out the excess seedlings when and where they occur.

Since a dry, infertile location should be used, it works in situations where little else will grow, and where the gardener does not wish to amend the soil. The soil in the cut-flower garden pictured has a base of yellow clay with some organic matter added to the top layer, which provides a shallow medium for annuals, while the clay helps to control the Queen Anne's lace.

Queen Anne's lace will also thrive as a meadow plant where a wildflower planting is desired. More and more people are turning their suburban back yards into meadows.

Once you have established Queen Anne's lace, the pleasure of using it in arrangements, either by itself or with other flowers, will amply justify raising it. And, if you are subjected to any sneers from garden snobs because you are growing a common wildflower—some may even call it a weed—try not to be too smug as you sweetly explain that *Daucus carota* is an important element in your efforts to help the environment by encouraging biodiversity. You might even drop the magic words "Integrated Pest Management."

Daucus carota
(daw'kus ka-ro'ta)
QUEEN ANNE'S LACE

White and magenta sweet Williams, with lamb's-ears to the left and a burgundy berberis on the right.

A "carnation" that's easy to grow: sweet Williams.

This very useful plant is technically a biennial but returns so readily from seed that it makes itself perennial whatever we call it. Sweet William blooms in dense clusters, displaying its upward-facing flowers for maximum show. This has made it a long-time favorite with gardeners. *D. barbatus* 'Indian Carpet' is a well-known series having one-inch-wide flowers supported on ten-inch stems beginning in late spring.

Blossoms come in white, light to dark pink, magenta, red, and coral-pink or salmon. The edges of some blossoms are lighter in color, the petals separated and fringed, combining to create a visual spinning effect like a pinwheel. The dense clusters further this effect, making a small number of plants highly visible. In the photograph, taken in early June, notice how the sweet Williams brighten the scene, although only a few plants were used.

Removing the old flowers as they deteriorate will encourage repeat blossoms. Fresh green foliage adds good texture as a background for the blossoms. The leaves are long, smooth-edged, lancelike, dark green, and run up the stems with a layering effect, ending with a terminating whorl, in all aspects looking like miniature corn plants. There is a tendency for the foliage to become sparse at the bottom; when this occurs, just cut it back after flowering.

D. barbatus does best in direct sun but will tolerate some shade, as in an eastern-facing position where it will receive morning light, then be out of the direct sun for the rest of the day. Sweet Williams require a more fertile and moist soil than do the other dianthus, but they give more flowers, too.

Sweet Williams can be purchased as plants or raised from seed to provide color when needed. With the color range available they can be incorporated into any color scheme. The setting photograph demonstrates how to use the magenta/burgundy shades of sweet William most effectively. Here it is planted with lamb's-ears and *Berberis thunbergii* 'Rose Glow'. The burgundy and white of the flowers, the burgundy of the shrub, and the white of the lamb's-ears' foliage make a pleasing scene.

Taller varieties can be found for cutting, but the shorter ones for borders are usually placed in the front. Grouped *en masse,* sweet Williams can give you the perfect carpet to brighten an area. I think they are best used where temporary color is needed, and then replaced with something else to bloom later—or, better yet, grown with another perennial that will take over the scene later on, such as *Veronica* 'Sunny Border Blue'.

Dianthus barbatus
(di-an'thus bar-ba'tus)
SWEET WILLIAM

'Bath's Pink' dianthus at the base of a light purple
German iris.

With its blue stems, this dark pink dianthus makes a
perfect companion for the blue nigella.

There are three species of garden pinks that I have used over a period of twenty years with success and found to be the most reliable for our area. *D. × allwoodii* (Allwood pinks) and *D. deltoides* (maiden pinks) seem to endure the worst of our wet winters and the heat our summers inflict upon them. *D. gratianopolitanus* 'Tiny Rubies' has proven itself over the years, too.

The flowers of garden pinks range from single to densely double, beginning with white and moving through shades of light pink to deep rose pink, ending with crimson. The edges are usually serrated, some being deeply fringed. 'Doris' and 'Helen' are probably the most popular cultivars from the *D. × allwoodii* group.

The blossoms are about one and a half inches in diameter, on stalks eight inches to one foot tall, making pinks an excellent cut flower. Most have a pleasing clove fragrance as well. Plants like 'Tiny Rubies' bloom so profusely that they hide the foliage in a dense cover. If kept disbudded, plants will continue to bloom sporadically through the season.

The accompanying close-up shows a double Allwood pink with the annual *Nigella damascena* (love-in-a-mist), blooming in June. These are planted at the foot of the white rose 'Iceberg' (not shown) for a pink-blue-white color scheme.

Foliage color in the dianthus family runs from blue-green to a frosty ice-blue. The individual leaves are long and narrow, and are as blue as the stems. *D. deltoides* forms a dense mat of clumping foliage, spreading low enough to pour over walls and cover large areas in the front of a perennial planting. *D. × allwoodii* creates small tufts of foliage that is usually bluer; it spreads, too, but not as densely.

One advantage of the Allwood pinks is their ability to grow well with only a half day of direct sun. An eastern-facing location is ideal. All dianthus can be used in direct sun all day. This keeps the crown dry, the way they like it, preventing moisture retention.

Good drainage is probably the most necessary factor for growing healthy dianthus, especially if attempted with only a half day of sun as mentioned above. If moisture is held around the crown, rot is guaranteed to set in. Drainage is also the determining factor for winter survival. With our wet winters, drainage is the one circumstance that determines hardiness—that and leaving them unmulched.

Because of the tendency for dianthus foliage to be short, they are best used with other low-growing perennials, or in front of taller ones. If taller perennials are used behind pinks, make sure they won't shade or fall on top of them. The foliage lasts all season and contributes a nice blue that looks attractive interrupting any edging, whether it be brick, stone, or grass.

> ⌒
> *Dianthus*
> (di-an'thus)
> GARDEN PINKS

Rising above the hedge in the foreground are 'Excelsior Strain' foxgloves.

'Apricot' foxglove, showing the freckled markings in the throat.

Here's another old garden favorite and biennial that liberally resows itself once established. *Digitalis purpurea*'s blossoms are striking, shaped like tubular bells. Flowers are light purple to magenta, a mixture of pinks and reds. The outsides of the blossoms carry the rich colors, while the inside throat is usually much lighter with brown spots. *D. p.* 'Alba' has the throat splotches and is pure white. At their tallest height of four feet foxgloves are unforgettable, their blossom stalks full of bells two feet down the stalk beginning in late May through early summer.

Plants of foxglove grow in a triangular formation, the leaves larger lower down and diminishing in size further up the stem. Leaf color is dull green with a fuzzy texture. The foliage can spread about one foot wide, the plants clumping together to form tight colonies.

Foxgloves are easy to grow, readily hardy for the Lower Midwest, doing best in partial shade but tolerating full sun if kept moist. The ones in the photograph face south but have the luxury of shade part of the day. They love plenty of organic matter mixed in the soil, leafmold being their favorite.

A related species currently becoming more available in our area is the beautiful *D. × mertonensis,* the strawberry foxglove, sometimes labeled 'Apricot'. A close-up photograph reveals the pastel strawberry color with the slight bronzing before opening. Adding this one will provide foxglove bloom in June and July.

Foxgloves are useful in a perennial planting for height relief, their tall spikes lifting up above other plants. Their color goes well with blues, whites, and other shades of pink and lavender. Given a place among other perennials they will enhance any garden.

Since foxgloves will occupy the space all season, they should have companions nearby if color is desired after they are finished blooming. I like them surrounded by forget-me-nots and blue hostas of all sizes, with a dark background, preferably green, to show off the blossoms. Brick or stone walls work well, too. Foxgloves also look good massed by themselves in an island bed.

There is a true perennial foxglove called *D. grandiflora* (*ambigua*)—not as showy, but a lovely pale yellow. It has smaller flowers, a shinier leaf, and blooms in June and July. You need several plants of *grandiflora* to make a good showing, but the pale yellow is handsome in the garden, especially with whites and purples.

Digitalis purpurea
(dij-i-ta'lis pur-pur'e-a)
FOXGLOVE

The petals of coneflower 'White Swan'
glow beneath the prominent cones.

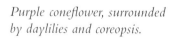

Purple coneflower, surrounded
by daylilies and coreopsis.

This perennial looks like a purple black-eyed Susan. It is native to the eastern United States, and can handle our hot summers with gusto. With its extended blooming period, this is one of the most carefree plants a gardener can use.

E. p. 'Bright Star'—one of the most common selections—is readily available from nurseries and mail order catalogs. The dark lavender-pink florets extend outward from the base of the brown and orange protruding cone, the orange center sitting like a pincushion above the daisylike petals. *E. p.* 'White Swan' does the same thing with pure white petals, making the orange pincushion even more striking.

The large blossoms, about three inches across, begin appearing in June and July, lasting well until frost. The flowers persist a long time and, after the petals fall off, leave behind the dramatic pincushion heads for winter interest if not cut down. As if this weren't enough, coneflower makes a superb cut flower to go with daisies, phlox, coreopsis, and other perennials that bloom at the same time.

Leaves are four to eight inches long and dark green, hanging on stems up to four feet tall. The foliage is somewhat coarse, but occupies the space in a planting without any blemishes until the blossoms begin to appear. The stems are sturdy and need no support.

Coneflower will thrive in full sun or light shade (four hours of direct sun with bright light the rest of the day). An eastern- or western-facing situation would be acceptable, too. Echinacea will also do well in a hot, dry location, which is easy enough to find in these parts.

If the soil drains well coneflower will tolerate a variety of soil textures. I have placed them in some clay soils with good results as long as drainage was satisfactory. This is a vigorous perennial that will settle in just about anywhere.

Either color of coneflower is good to use with phlox, daylilies, daisies, coreopsis, and many other perennials, in large clumps in a mixed shrub and perennial planting, or beside peonies to provide color after the peonies have blossomed. They make a bold contrast in shape and texture with Russian sage, and the lavender-pink coneflower is great with the sage's white foliage and blue flowers.

> ꙩ
>
> *Echinacea purpurea*
> (ek-i-na'se-a pur-pur-e'a)
> PURPLE CONEFLOWER

*Impressive bicolor blossoms of
Epimedium versicolor.*

*Epimedium in the foreground of a woodland
garden; Christmas rose on the right and a
wildflower, purple phacelia, to the left and
behind.*

The best of ground covers for the shade, epimediums contribute both a soft elegance and a practical function. Their foliage serves throughout the growing year, long after the clusters of blossoms are gone, and is as handsome as the flowers. The new leaves are shaped like yellow-green hearts with a mahogany edging and a delicate serration along the margins. The plants are small and remain low to the ground. Twelve inches is about as tall as any of the cultivars stand, and they spread just as wide.

Gardens are still bare when the first epimedium flowers make their appearance in April. The small clusters of jewellike blossoms, in shades of red, yellow, pink and yellow, or white, come up on delicate stems well before the foliage begins opening out. *E. × rubrum* has dark red petals and a white cross layered against the underside. *E. × versicolor* looks like a miniature daffodil, with its tiny cup and reflexed petals.

A compelling reason to start growing epimedium tomorrow is their ability to withstand not only shade, but dry shade. They even do well in competition with tree roots, something one hesitates to ask of most perennials, let alone such a beautiful one.

In direct sun, epimediums wilt in the heat of the day, but they continue to thrive if they are given plenty of moisture to compensate. If you plant them under trees, be sure the trees are limbed up and that bright light is reflected around the base. Epimedium foliage will look its richest in the partial shade of an eastern-facing location.

For maximum growth the soil should be rich in organic matter and kept moist. I can't stress this enough, for epimedium is rather slow to increase. That combined with its current popularity makes epimedium expensive. I have seen one-gallon pots going for $12. If the pot is full and the contents can be divided into five to seven pieces to spread around, it is not so bad, but I am unhappy when I see a retail nursery offering pots this size, each containing a little scrap that looks as if it had been planted six months ago. This is not how to buy a perennial, or, to be more direct, to sell one.

In any case, don't let the price discourage you. This refined plant can be used effectively in ways other than as a ground cover that don't require vast numbers. (You might also want to choose yellow or red varieties, which seem to be the most vigorous.) When conditions are appropriate, in clumps of three to five it makes an attractive edging plant in the front of a perennial border. Along walks and driveways it brings much-needed relief to their hard surfaces. The foliage is a good companion with spring bulbs, anchoring the taller flowers with an attractive base. And of course epimedium looks wonderful in woodland gardens with ferns, hostas, and snakeroot. Where to use this charming perennial is limited only by one's imagination.

Epimedium
(ep-i-me'de-um)
BARRENWORT

The large blossom heads and dark stems of 'Gateway'.

An improved form of Joe-Pye-weed, Giant Eupatorium 'Gateway' creates a passageway with Hydrangea 'Annabelle' on the right.

Difficult to miss at seven feet or more, our five species of Joe-Pye-weed can be seen in fall blooming along roads and fields. One of them, *Eupatorium maculatum,* Spotted Joe-Pye-weed, is a plant of northern and eastern wetlands. Its cultivar 'Gateway' is smaller. It is a giant in the garden nonetheless, and very showy come late summer.

The size as well as the color of the large flower heads will lend stature to any garden; they are overwhelming both up close and from a distance. Eighteen-inch-wide blossom clusters ride six feet tall on deep red stems. Individual florets are wine red at the base with wisps of pink, hair-thin petals spraying out at the top. From a distance, the wine red blends with lighter pink petals, so that the mass looks pink. Elliptical, serrated dark green leaves move in whorls all the way up the deep red stems, with midribs of the same wine color.

'Gateway' responds well to full sun and plenty of moisture, and grows to an impressive size even in one season. The mature plants in the photograph have reached their maximum height of six feet, which took about three years. They are growing in a clay soil and get adequate moisture. The results are evident.

Joe-Pye-weed needs bold companions in the garden. Placed against a wall, as shown in the photograph, it displays a strong presence. The brick wall makes a good background, better defining the tall plant. Just to the left is a sixteen-foot juniper, and to its right is a kousa dogwood. Creating an entrance to a lower garden, *E. m.* 'Gateway' frames one side of the walk, while the other is defined by *Hydrangea arborescens* 'Annabelle', another large-blossomed shrub.

'Gateway' is so imposing it can be placed in the back or middle of a planting with outstanding results. Consider using it around streams or ponds for a natural setting. Shrubs like the variegated red-twig dogwood, with its red stems and green and white foliage, would be excellent companions.

Try it or one of the other Joe-Pye-weeds to anchor a corner of a garage, or any building for that matter. It is dense enough to be used as a screen along property lines, or to hide any unsightly mess you are tired of seeing.

Eupatorium maculatum
'Gateway'
(u-pa-tor'ee-um mak-u-la'tum)
JOE-PYE-WEED

Maidenhair fern dances at the edge of a pool.

Delicate fingers of maidenhair fern in cool shade.

The lacy fronds of maidenhair ferns belie their toughness as they rise up in a graceful swirl to dance on the air. Primordial yet sophisticated, they are hardy to zone 3.

Adiantum pedatum is finely textured and lends a soft touch to a shady planting. New fronds come out lime green, then age to a darker green with a slight blue cast. The fronds branch into several segments at the top of the stem, spreading out like a flat green hand made of feathers. The wiry stems and frond ribs are almost black, reaching straight up off the ground to a height of eighteen inches. The plants will spread about as wide, colonizing under favorable conditions.

Maidenhair fern grows naturally in a woodland setting and on moist hillsides. Moisture is critical when using this native in the urban garden—urban meaning anything outside the woods. In such situations I've used it successfully in full shade (no direct sun but bright light). Soil texture high in organic content (to retain needed moisture) is another requirement.

An eastern-facing location is also good for this ancient fern, one with three to four hours of softer morning sun. In this situation, mix it with dicentras, hostas, and spiderworts for a great combination.

I like using maidenhair around pools or any shaded body of water. If planting under trees, be sure the soil is deep enough to give the fern the moisture it requires. When I construct pools with plantings under trees, I usually add organic compost or peat, or, best of all, imitate maidenhair's natural setting and work in leafmold.

There is nothing like maidenhair fern to soften a shady planting. Add it alongside hellebores (Lenten or Christmas roses) for a good contrast in texture. Or put maidenhair near some blue hostas, such as *sieboldiana* 'Elegans', in a woodland garden. The blue of the hosta foliage enhances the blue in the maidenhair fronds. Then add sparkle with a white annual forget-me-not.

Epimedium is another perennial with bluish foliage that is a good companion for maidenhair. Seeing the tight little fists of fragile-looking epimedium stems and the tender fiddleheads of maidenhair pushing up through the soil together in the spring is a joy not to be missed.

FERNS

Adiantum pedatum

(ad-e-an'tum ped-ah'tum)

NORTHERN
MAIDENHAIR FERN

Lady fern arching its fronds.

*Providing a background for the sundial:
the fine texture of lady fern.*

86

A finely textured fern that will brighten the shade garden with its upright elegance and triangular wings of translucent green, the vigorous lady fern can be placed in a variety of settings.

Light enters the fern fronds and seems to illuminate the chlorophyll from within, displaying sharp lime green foliage that darkens to a musty green with maturity. The fronds usually grow up to three feet tall, twice divided (bipinnate), on dark brown stems.

The foliage is strong, standing straight from a basal clump, then arching over gracefully. Looking down on the center in the close-up photograph one sees three fronds coming together, then bending away, like dolphins lifting out of the water simultaneously, each doing a backwards dive.

This is one of the best ferns for Lower Midwest gardens because it tolerates different types of soil. I've planted lady fern in a variety of soils without amending any of them and had good success. Of course, it will do best in rich humus, but will put up with less than ideal situations.

I've read that it will tolerate dry shade for short periods of time, not really proliferating, but maintaining a sound presence—which sometimes is good enough. It is one of the easier ferns to grow, given its range of soil tolerance and the fact that it will do well in sun or shade.

The native setting is a woodland site, which of course can be replicated as closely as possible; if such a site isn't available, just plant lady fern in some shade, or in an eastern-facing location, and water moderately—she can handle it.

According to one well-known reference, the color of lady fern is not the best of greens to work with, but I think it blends readily (especially when fronds first unfold) with golden and yellow-variegated hostas, with yellow corydalis laced throughout. The delicate texture of both the fern and the corydalis works well to counteract the boldness of the hosta foliage.

Lady fern makes a good companion for rhododendrons and azaleas, spreading under and around them as a ground cover. Put them all together under high-canopied trees, among rocks and large stones, for a natural-looking environment.

Athyrium filix-femina
(a-ther'ree-um fi'liks-fem'i-na)
LADY FERN

Japanese painted fern nestled among blue blossoms of ajuga, brunnera, and forget-me-nots.

The red and silver of Japanese painted fern, enhanced by forget-me-nots.

Probably the most colorful fern there is, *Athyrium niponicum* 'Pictum' (= *A. goeringianum* 'Pictum') offers the greatest possibility among ferns to bring color to shady areas. If you are used to "ferns as usual," this one will be a pleasant surprise.

As its new fronds unfold, one sees deep burgundy veins with silver and green markings on the foliage. The fronds, which can reach up to eighteen inches, are deeply divided and dissected, with the silver-splashed coloration varying from plant to plant. It has deservedly become a "darling" among gardeners in the past ten years or so.

The plants take shape in clump form, usually tripling or better in size each season. As the fiddleheads open up to maturity they become more horizontal to the ground, keeping the fern height to the maximum eighteen inches. Plants will vary not only in coloration but in height. There is also a smaller cultivar of the painted fern with fronds half the size.

Japanese painted fern thrives in moist humus that never dries out. It will tolerate full shade as well as the half shade associated with an eastern-facing location, receiving three to four hours of direct sun, then shade for the remainder of the day. I've had *A. niponicum* in eastern- and western-facing locations with equal success.

It is a good companion for hostas, other ferns, and spring bulbs. An unparalleled combination is 'Pictum' with *Ajuga* 'Burgundy Glow'. They share a compatible tricoloration, the fern being the taller and darker, and the ajuga the shorter and lighter.

Coral impatiens is also good with this fern. I am now waiting for an opportunity to use Japanese painted fern with a wine-red impatiens I have seen in local nurseries. The similar dark reds should be stunning with all the silver in the fronds of this unique fern.

I was first introduced to this fern long before it became popular, thanks to an article read by chance in *The New York Times*. A man in Cincinnati named Tim Morehouse was raising ferns from spores he had germinated in his basement over winter. I called him, later went to visit, and we became fast friends.

Tim showed me ferns I didn't think possible—ferns with segments that crossed each other as if they weren't sure which way to grow off the stems, fronds that had small round circles of green along the stems, until, reaching the end, they exploded in a rush of crested fullness. The former is the 'Victoria' fern, while the latter carries the apt name of 'Tattingfern'. I loved ferns before I got there—after visiting Tim I found myself in an expanded new world!

Athyrium niponicum **'Pictum'**
(a-ther'ree-um ni-pon'i-kum)
JAPANESE PAINTED FERN

*Tall fronds of glade fern stand in a shady bed
behind an ancient dogwood tree.*

The rippling fronds of glade fern.

90

This American native is another fern that strays from the usual image of a "fern." Sometimes four feet tall, it has the grace and form of a slim dancer. I first saw it growing in Harriett Holladay's garden in Lexington, Kentucky, in a small colony behind her garage, and was immediately impressed with its size. It took me several years before I could put a name to this fern, but it wasn't long before I had some in my own garden; and, thanks to Harriett's generosity, it tended to spread to other gardens whenever I described the luscious thing to their owners.

Athyrium pycnocarpum (some authorities spell it *pycnocarpum*) is bold because of its height and yet delicate because of the slim and wavy fronds. The foliage looks like a tall version of the indoor Boston fern. The large fiddleheads unfurl into a rosette pattern, standing vertically, a vivid yellow-green. As the fronds mature, they darken but remain a fresh, vibrant green.

The plants in the photograph are facing east but receive sun until about three in the afternoon. They have tolerated this part-day hot sun because their roots never dry out where they are located. It is most necessary that they have a damp site.

One easy way to have such a site is to dig a shallow depression in a shady part of the garden, preferably at the base of an incline or at least below the normal garden level. This done, you will have an area to hold much-needed moisture for glade fern and other moisture-loving perennials.

The glade fern will colonize nicely, spreading yearly at a moderate rate. If given the good humus soil that is necessary, it will proliferate into surrounding perennials if not checked at least every two years or so. *A. pycnocarpum* cannot be called invasive, but is vigorous enough to spread over an area if allowed to. As with most perennials, being divided periodically encourages new growth, especially if it is in competition with other plants.

In a shade border, a perennial that will bring some height into a planting of mainly horizontal materials is to be cherished. Glade fern performs this function in bright shade as well as in more sun, as noted above.

American glade fern is great to toss in with other ferns to have one that stands above the others. The colony in the photograph is planted with hostas, arum, Solomon's seal, and a patch of forget-me-nots. These make good companions; so would snakeroot, lilies, geraniums, campanulas, and shrubs such as azaleas, mountain laurels, and rhododendrons.

I've always thought they would look wonderful coming up out of a flat-growing cover like ivy or pachysandra, shooting up from the vast pool of green like verdant geysers.

*Athyrium
pycnocarpum*
(a-ther'ree-um pic-no-carp'um)
AMERICAN GLADE FERN

91

*Light green fronds of cinnamon fern
unfurl among silver 'Herman's Pride',
a non-invasive lamiastrum.*

*Here, cinnamon fern softens the brick and
makes a setting for the sculpture.*

A distinctive-looking fern because of its woolly, fertile fronds, sticking up separately from the other green fronds. As a native of our eastern United States, *Osmunda cinnamomea* will flourish in most places with plenty of moisture, doing even better than you might wish.

The cinnamon fern has chartreuse fronds from beginning to maturity. They are pinnately divided and can become three feet tall. These green fronds form an oblong diamond shape, the base of the frond narrow, spreading to its widest at the center, then narrowing again toward the tip. The fertile fronds, which carry the reddish-brown spores, look like cinnamon sticks, hence its common name.

Some references suggest that *O. cinnamomea* needs an acid soil, but I've had success with this fern in limestone-based clay. It has immense vigor. I've seen it suddenly appear on the opposite side of a seven-foot-high brick wall without any human assistance. It will spread rampantly in a moist, shady site, and care must be taken when placing it in the garden. It will also work just as well in the sun if the site is wet, or under an automated sprinkler system.

For this reason the cinnamon fern makes an excellent ground cover for a moist location. It also makes the cinnamon fern a good perennial to place beside pools and streams, assuming that nothing else is wanted in the same spot.

Its yellow-green coloration is good with gold and yellow hostas, blue ones, and those variegated with both colors. Hostas are probably the best choice as companion perennials with this fern. Even with the strong spread of hosta foliage there is no guarantee that the cinnamon fern won't get in their way.

Another use could be with rhododendrons or other shrubs, tying the shrubs together with other elements of the garden. Instead of competing with these larger plants the ferns would form a healthy partnership.

A tougher character for deep shade can't be found. If you need a fern glade in a hurry, this is the fern to try regardless of soil. Place it in a wet area and be ready to let it take over.

∞

Osmunda cinnamomea
(os-mun'da sin-na-mo'me-a)
CINNAMON FERN

Christmas fern comes up through yellow archangel in a shade garden.

Standing straight up on the right is Christmas fern, sharing the shade with the taller snakeroot behind it. Jack-in-the-pulpit foliage can be seen at center.

Probably the most common fern grown in our area, *Polystichum acrostichoides* is another eastern North American native. It's called evergreen by textbooks and nurseries, and does technically stay green through the winter, in a matted, blobby sort of way. In the Lower Midwest, though, it is not a plant to count on for year-round visual appeal.

Nonetheless, Christmas fern does deserve to be used in the shade garden. I would not think of doing without it, although I wouldn't place it in a high-visibility area. Its dark green, lance-shaped fronds have a leathery texture, and reach two feet tall. The plants make dense, mounding clumps, spreading two feet.

In both heavy and light shade, they do well, covering and growing successfully. They will tolerate more sun than the ideal partial-shade scenario if they never dry out, but are more carefree in humus soil and a woodland setting. A site where they are exposed to direct morning light will serve nicely too.

Christmas fern is actually a very easy fern to grow when given shade and adequate moisture. It does require well-drained soil, but I've planted it in some clay soils, adding organic matter only in the hole at planting time. As long as your soil drains well, try some.

Christmas ferns are good to use with spring bulbs and other shade perennials because they stay in neat clumps, not overwhelming nearby companions as some other ferns do. Seeing small bulbs like Siberian squill, snowdrops, and crocus coming up through Christmas fern's new fiddleheads in the spring is a treat.

I like mixing Christmas fern with astilbes for a textural contrast in a shade planting, or with variegated or yellow hostas for color contrast. In this way they can be used as part of a ground cover, or, planted in large quantities, be used alone.

Not my least favorite use for Christmas fern would be as the third element in a tree–shrub–ground cover situation. *P. acrostichoides* looks good under many different shrubs and trees, provided that conditions are suitable for their growth and that they are not in total darkness.

Incidentally, the leathery fronds do an exceptional job used as greenery in arrangements—something that makes it a greater asset than if it were truly evergreen.

Polystichum acrostichoides
(po-lis'ti-kum a-kros-ti-koy'des)
CHRISTMAS FERN

Tiny white flowers sprinkled across sweet woodruff in a shady spot under cinnamon fern.

The fine texture of sweet woodruff, foreground, is the perfect foil for the heavier hosta foliage.

This little plant has tiny, fragrant white flowers, held in loose clusters at the top of short stems. Blossoms are only a quarter of an inch wide, but showy in May and June. The foliage gives off a pleasant scent when crushed. In Europe it has been used for centuries to flavor wines and liqueurs. The lance-shaped leaves, with fine-toothed margins and hairy tips, are whorled around the square stems, adding to sweet woodruff's distinctive appearance.

G. odoratum is useful as a ground cover for either deep or partial shade. The plants spread into a fine-textured, delicate mat, and light reflected from the shiny, dark green leaves brightens shady areas. To be at its best, it should have constant moisture, although it will do adequately without it, and soil needs to drain sufficiently so that water will not be held for long periods. It can take three or four hours of morning sun at most. This is a matting, shallow-rooted perennial that is transplanted like sod—preferably in large chunks, otherwise in smaller plugs.

Woodruff likes moist, shady areas under high-skirted shrubs, effectively tying these larger elements to the buildings and serving as an attractive mulch. Or it can be used to decorate the edges of shady walkways, spilling over to soften the hard lines. It is the perfect complement to ferns or hostas and looks good with daffodils growing up through it. It looks good in the wildflower garden, planted with trillium.

I concede there are many better plants for sunny places. But keep sweet woodruff in the shade and you won't be disappointed with this little jewel.

Galium odoratum
(gay'li-um o-do-ra'tum)
SWEET WOODRUFF

There's not a better blue for the garden than 'Johnson's Blue'.

The spectacular 'Johnson's Blue' geranium, seen beneath yellow-variegated dogwoods.

Cranesbills are true *hardy* geraniums, as opposed to the ones (that are really pelargoniums) we buy each summer to plant in porch containers. After experiencing the true geranium, and not having to buy it year after year, you might gain an entirely new respect for the word "geranium." Of course, one kind does not replace the other because cultural requirements are not similar.

Hardy geranium blossoms range from white to pink, through magenta (with plenty of purples), to the featured blue. Some, like *Geranium himalayense,* have darker veins lacing through the lighter-colored petals. As a group they excel at flowering for a long period of time, look good after they bloom, and require little maintenance. What's more, hardy geraniums can really light up the fall garden with yellow or—in the case of 'Johnson's Blue'—blazing scarlet foliage.

G. × 'Johnson's Blue' is a rich, deep blue (as blue as they come), and usually blossoms for me, in Lexington, for about two months. This is a long bloom time for a perennial. The only problem with 'Johnson's Blue' is that it tends to sprawl a bit. Regardless, it stands well enough to create a showy display, as shown in the photograph.

The foliage of hardy geranium is as interesting as the blossoms. Leaves are deeply lobed and usually divided into five parts, but some are hairy and some are aromatic (*G. macrorrhizum,* the bigroot geranium). Most of the geraniums we want to use in the Lower Midwest top out at two feet (for anything taller than that, staking is required, which is too much work), and are used where shorter masses are desired.

Cranesbills are vigorous, showing an adaptability to different soil types, with drainage being the biggest factor for success. These geraniums can tolerate full sun where there are cool summers, which might be possible in the extreme northern areas of the Lower Midwest; where summers are hot, hardy geraniums do their best in partial shade or dappled light.

Some hardy geraniums form small clumps as they grow, and some can roam large areas as a ground cover. The species types like our North American native, *G. maculatum,* will spread around nicely, while 'Johnson's Blue' stays in a smaller area. Don't be put off thinking of them as a ground cover because of expense. They divide easily, and, planted at one- or two-foot intervals and given good moisture, will cover an area in two to three years.

The 'Johnson's Blue' depicted here has been growing with success in a clay-based soil for years. With this adaptability, it is a designer's dream plant because its bright blue color enhances any planting.

All the above-mentioned geraniums are impressive with other perennials in a border, massed together as a ground cover, or placed along walks and walls. In a border they are usually placed close to the front or in the middle, depending on the border's width.

> ❧
>
> *Geranium* ×
> *'Johnson's Blue'*
> (je-ra'ni-um)
> CRANESBILL,
> HARDY GERANIUM

99

The clear white markings of Japanese silver grass.

Japanese silver grass making a fountain spray in a perennial bed.

I never succumbed to the grass craze that struck our continent a few years ago, maybe because here in the Midwest we seem to have plenty of grass in our surrounding fields. I like using grasses mostly with other perennials, and only when the situation calls for them, and I treat them like any other perennial. I confess that Japanese silver grass is my favorite.

Grasses do flower, in their way, and this one has creamy-pink tassels usually beginning in October. The stately plumes stand up slightly above the foliage, bending over like silky water.

Better value is given by the foliage, which remains good looking all season and provides beautiful texture and color. *Miscanthus sinensis* 'Variegatus', one of the most useful grasses, has beautiful green blades edged with white. All this white inspired the common name of silver grass, but, practically speaking, light green is how it appears visually in the garden. Japanese silver grass stands up to six feet in a loose, arching form that is dense enough to screen unsightly areas.

Plenty of sun is its main requirement. It is not particular about soil, as can be seen in the accompanying photograph—this one stands in clay.

M. s. 'Variegatus' is a very bold plant; in the photo mentioned above, it is hiding the ever-present cable junction box for the neighborhood. A little of this grass does the job and creates a nice background for the cut-flower garden.

Because of its size, it can screen garbage cans from a sitting area on a terrace while at the same time creating vertical interest for the garden. It is impressive enough to be planted with shrubs of all sizes, especially with vertical forms such as taxus, holly, or junipers behind it providing a dark green background for its foliage.

Silver grass can be used nicely in the rear of perennial plantings, itself creating the background, contrasting in texture with Russian sage, baby's breath, or any other tall and showy perennials.

Quickly becoming another favorite is *M. s.* 'Morning Light', another green and white striped grass with narrower leaves. It is just as effective as 'Variegatus' but, having thinner foliage, it appears lighter. 'Morning Light' is shorter also—four to five feet tall, with blossom stalks up to six feet. It looks especially effective in large urns.

One of the best reasons to use grasses is for their low-maintenance appeal. Leave their foliage and blossom stalks standing all winter for visual interest—something we can all use more of at that time of year.

Fine foliage and soft flower heads of
fountain grass add up to great texture.

Dwarf fountain grass at its best with
coppery-pink flower spikes.

Whereas Japanese silver grass is interesting all season long, *Pennisetum alopecuroides* is really at its best only when it flowers. But when it does, it is impressive.

Flowering stalks top out at four feet, the slender bottlebrush spike consuming the top seven inches. The bristle-type seed heads spray outward, giving the plant an even, round shape. The reddish-brown bristles have a creamy center. The overall effect in August and September is like white candles with a maroon halo.

The leaves are slender, arching over to form compact mounds three feet tall and three feet wide. Overall the foliage lends a bright green, bushy texture to a planting.

Full sun is required for fountain grass to flower in the garden. It will grow in light shade, but in that case may not flower, and I wouldn't risk that. Any soil that drains well can be tolerated.

A green background gives the flower spikes better definition, as can be seen in the photographs with the arborvitae on the left. Its other companion in the foreground is *Hypericum frondosum* (St. John's wort).

Fountain grass has reddish-brown seed heads that look best grouped with other perennials in a planting unless you purposely want a savannah-type appearance. It makes a good anchor in a border because of its mass. The finely textured foliage blends nicely with that of German iris, Siberian iris, and daylilies. For a contrasting combination try grouping fountain grass with phlox (especially pink phlox), Japanese anemones, and of course sedum.

My favorite placement would be grouped with *Hydrangea paniculata* 'Grandiflora', where the maturing rose-pink blossoms of the hydrangea would complement the reddish-brown blossoms of the grass. Pairing these two with the red-twig shrub dogwood would further the blending of reds, and be an interesting contrast in form as well.

The foliage will add interest to the winter garden if left standing, the thin blades turning a light brown, providing shape and form. One of the best characteristics of fountain grass is its tolerance of wind. Fountain grass could be used to advantage here as a buffer or screen.

ᘓ

Pennisetum alopecuroides
(pen-i-se'tum a-lo-pek-u-roy'deez)
FOUNTAIN GRASS

Its crisp green and white leaves tempt gardeners to mistakenly plant ribbon grass without barriers.

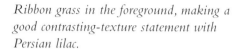

Ribbon grass in the foreground, making a good contrasting-texture statement with Persian lilac.

This is often the first ornamental grass to be used in gardens in our area, and it might be the last: gardeners who place this grass where it can grow unrestricted will likely be so discouraged they may never try another.

The loose flowers are a creamy pale pink, not particularly attractive, and insignificant compared to the foliage. Leaves are brightly striped in white and green, twelve inches long, and wrap around the stem at intervals. Each leaf curves outward on the stem, somewhat like bamboo. The vivid colors can really liven up some types of plantings.

Phalaris arundinacea 'Picta' foliage is so pretty you might be tempted to put it in the perennial border or mix it with other plants, but don't do it! This grass is really not for the perennial border, not even planted in a sunken container. The long runners are not to be trusted. They would just as soon climb over the top of any container you choose.

The green and white foliage remains good-looking throughout the summer. Somewhere around late summer, when it does turn an ugly brown, treat this perennial like any other grass—cut it all the way down to the ground with clippers; or, easier yet, use a mower. Fresh new leaves will return in no time. And if once doesn't rejuvenate it sufficiently, mow it again.

Ribbon grass is adaptable to various soils and is one of the few grasses that will thrive in hot and dry situations. Infertile soil will restrict its voracious running habit. It tolerates direct sun or half sun, and reigns supreme along stream banks—that is, if you want nothing else with it.

A good use for ribbon grass is in hot areas along driveways and walks. Heat absorbed from concrete or blacktop drives won't slow it down even a little. Such areas are usually very dry and have hard edges that ribbon grass will gladly help smooth out.

Wherever it is used, *P. a.* 'Picta' will usually be weed free; there are not many weeds that can compete with it. This fact can be used to advantage when ribbon grass is planted in a hot area that needs total coverage. Just be sure to avoid using it anywhere near the lawn. It will get in there and outgrow the grass!

For a long time I've wanted to try placing this vicious grass together with cinnamon fern along a creek bank to see which would outgrow the other. Or maybe my suspicion is correct, and they are perfectly compatible friends. With their different textures, shapes, and colors, they would be terrific together.

ᘒ

Phalaris arundinacea
'Picta'
(fal'ar-iss a-run-di-na'se-a)
RIBBON GRASS,
GARDENER'S GARTERS

Gypsophila 'Bristol Fairy' in a raised bed with Russian sage and iris foliage to the left and lavender in the foreground.

A cloud of baby's breath.

When *Gypsophila paniculata* has a good year in the garden, it is memorable. At the height of flowering it is like a white cloud come to earth to share with us an ethereal mist of beauty. *G. p.* 'Bristol Fairy' is the best known, with double white blossoms. The flowers are tiny but numerous, beginning in June. From the close-up photograph you can see how dense the flowers are on the leafless stems—there are literally thousands—and it has the capacity to continue blooming if kept cut back. Baby's breath is long-lasting in arrangements of cut flowers. It will look delightful even after it dries.

The foliage is rather insignificant—short, lance-shaped leaves that are a pleasant grayish-green, borne on thin, skeletal branches that appear much too fragile to lift the load of blossoms up to four feet tall. Pretty in its own right, the foliage provides a strong supporting framework, holding the scene in a planting while awaiting the great eclipse of blossom.

Baby's breath needs full sun with soil that drains well. The best growth I've seen has been in raised beds, such as those illustrated. This method of raised-bed culture will satisfy the "well-drained soil" requirement as no other can. Without it, *G. paniculata* has a difficult time coming through our simultaneously wet and cold winters (most winters in the southern parts of the Lower Midwest are like this; the northern parts should have better success with it). Also try raised-bed gardening for other perennials that are equally demanding of good drainage.

A raised bed requires extensive labor. An easier way, for either an existing planting or a new one, is to dig a deep hole and fill it with pea gravel, add some soil, and then plant the baby's breath on top.

The soil pH for the baby's breath pictured here is probably close to neutral, having been slightly alkaline to begin with; peat moss was added when the raised bed was filled to increase the acidity. I've read three different recommendations for the best pH levels for *Gypsophila:* acid, neutral, and alkaline (this covers all the possibilities); but as you can see, it is doing well in this situation.

With its spherical habit, baby's breath is one of the best plants for creating a light relief in any grouping of perennials. It is nice with vertically oriented things, such as Russian sage, grasses, and iris (to name a few), and can also be used as the dominant plant in a smaller-scale grouping, with lavender, coreopsis, salvia, coralbells (as seen in the illustration), lady's-mantle, and geraniums. Underplanted with bulbs, the baby's breath will hide their deteriorating foliage.

Gypsophila also comes in pink, which does not do as well as the white varieties. A new white cultivar called 'Perfecta' is supposedly a larger-flowering double with more vigor than 'Bristol Fairy'. Vigor is one of the most important characteristics to look for in a perennial—it enables the gardener to stretch the parameters of its recommended usage successfully.

Gypsophila paniculata
(jip-sof'i-la pan-ik-u-la'ta)
BABY'S BREATH

The Lenten rose showing off in April.

Unforgettable white blossoms of the
hellebore called the Christmas rose.

Interest in hellebores is growing, and so is the number of available hybrids, but the two best known are still the Christmas rose and the Lenten rose. *Helleborus niger* can bloom at Christmas, but it usually waits until very early spring in the Lower Midwest. December, February, or March—whenever it blooms, it is worth having. *H. orientalis* is the Lenten rose, blooming later than the Christmas rose with a flower that is more striking because of its reddish-purple hue. Both are an enormous asset in the winter and spring garden for their attractive foliage and early blossoms, with *H. orientalis* the easier to grow.

The Christmas rose has five single, pure white sepals that are distinctly separated, facing outward and singly on the stem, creating the flower, up to six inches wide and usually freckled inside with dark purple-maroon. Deep in the center is a flush of lime green that sets off the yellow stamens.

The Lenten rose can be white and is sometimes mistaken for the Christmas rose. It usually has deep burgundy rose–colored flowers with cream and light green running through both sides of the sepal. Some flowers are lighter than others; some have flowers of several colors on the same plant; and all usually have distinct freckles on the inside. This is all said because you can be sure that every plant has different coloration, so, if possible, choose them in bloom. Both species have a multitude of pale yellow or cream-colored stamens that protrude from the center, adding to their appeal.

The foliage, with its thick, leathery segments, is as interesting as the flowers. Segment division is deep and usually in seven to nine parts, giving hellebores a unique-looking leaf. If you need to identify either when out of bloom, *H. orientalis* has better-defined teeth along the leaf margin.

One of the best perennials for shade—full shade or half shade—hellebores are in a class of their own. But keep them out of the hot midday sun. Hellebores prefer humusy soil, but I have found them tolerant of less, if the soil drains and stays moist.

Either of these hellebores should be located in a prominent spot: close to the front of a planting, along a walk, or, if you have only one plant, next to the house. Given a protected situation, the foliage can remain green all winter. Usually what happens here is that the shade they have enjoyed during the growing season disappears during the winter, resulting in the hot sun burning the foliage. When this occurs, cut it back in the spring and new leaves will appear.

I love to plant hellebores where they will come up with narcissus, grape hyacinths, *Anemone blanda,* and forget-me-nots. Include snakeroot, ferns, and hostas to have a plethora of foliage texture and blossom for a lush shade garden all year. Both hellebores are especially nice with some of the smaller yellow hostas such as 'Kabitan', a miniature with short, linear leaves that provide good contrast in texture and color, but most importantly are in suitable scale.

Helleborus
(hell-e-bor'us)
CHRISTMAS ROSE,
LENTEN ROSE

Yellow 'Stella d'Oro' daylily looks great with the globe blue spruce and a spot of white lamb's-ears.

Is it any wonder gardeners get lost in daylilies like 'Corryton Pink'?

110

Probably God's favorite plant, judging by the vast variety hybridized and sold. Most catalogs have a special section for daylilies because of their numbers. Your grandmother probably grew the tall orange "ditch lily," *Hemerocallis fulva,* or the earlier, shorter, scented yellow, *H. flava.* The color range has been increased tremendously since these two species were first brought to America. Some of my favorites are the pinks, salmons, and near-whites. Finding a favorite color is not difficult with daylilies. At peak bloom time, simply visit one of the Lower Midwest nurseries that specialize in them and see what appeals to you.

The foliage resembles tall, thick grass. The blades come out of the crown wider at the base, becoming more narrow further up, tapering to a point at the tip. Plants form bushy clumps, arching outward and creating a perfect base to display the vertical stalks of flowers. Foliage height ranges from eight inches to 2 1/2 feet, with the dwarfs' flower size in proportion to the leaves.

The blossoms are large, spectacular trumpets, facing upward and outward, on stalks up to 4 feet in height, depending upon the cultivar. Thick, leafless stems called scapes support the flower clusters, with each flower lasting only for a day. If you choose carefully from early to late-blooming cultivars, you can have daylilies in bloom from late May well into August and September.

There are early and late-blooming cultivars, and then there is 'Stella d'Oro', the current monarch of the daylily kingdom. Only eleven inches tall, she blooms profusely, beginning in June for us, and continues intermittently for the rest of the season.

Daylilies come in dark black-red; orange and yellow combinations; purple; peach with raspberry rings in the throat; ruffles on the petal margins; striped petals; green throats—everything except blue and pure white. While most hybridizers have concentrated on achieving wonderful new colors, efforts to breed for cultivars with longer blooming times and more blossoms like 'Stella d'Oro' are much needed.

Daylily diversity doesn't stop with color. These rugged perennials can adapt to a wide range of soil types. They thrive in some of the worst soils and conditions possible, even clay, provided that it doesn't hold water for long periods. They will even compete with tree roots in half shade. Four to five hours' direct sun gives them enough light to bloom well.

Daylilies can be massed under high-canopied trees, used with other perennials, grouped in collections to bloom most of the season, or grown in containers on the terrace. There are untold ways to use them, they are so versatile and carefree. Try a few hundred next season and see if you don't agree.

Hemerocallis
(hem-er-o-kal'is)
DAYLILY

Heuchera 'Palace Purple'.

The burgundy foliage of 'Palace Purple' in the bottom right corner is a welcome relief from all the green. Baptisia blooms at left.

Heuchera micrantha 'Palace Purple' has gained a significant place among coralbells and in American gardens in the typical way plants gain notoriety: because they have a distinguishing feature that sets them apart from other species in the same family. Sometimes such a plant is really worthy and sometimes not. 'Palace Purple', which comes to us from western North America, deserves special attention because of its unique foliage color.

Describing 'Palace Purple' foliage doesn't do it justice. You really need to see it in the garden. Among green-foliaged plants, the dark leaves look like a large purple ivy with a green underlayer showing through. This color alone sets it apart, and it spreads an impressive eighteen inches in height and width.

A purple-leaved plant couldn't have a better blossom color than white. The white flowers are tiny, as is typical of coralbells, and hang in dainty clusters beginning halfway up the thin eighteen-inch stems. Blossoms appear in late spring to early summer in our area.

The hybridizers are now busy producing dozens of other heuchera cultivars with ornamental foliage. If they could also produce the range of flower colors available on "ordinary" coralbells, what a show we would have!

'Palace Purple' is at home in half shade, an east-facing location being ideal. The optimum soil will be full of organic matter. Clay soils will slow growth some, but as long as it gets good drainage, 'Palace Purple' will put up with adverse conditions.

Coralbells generally need dividing about every three years to maintain their vigor. The crowns become woody during this time, and growth becomes sparse. Remove the areas of woody crown in spring or fall, where there is no growth, and replant the sections with foliage. If the crowns should heave up out of the ground in winter, I usually press them gently back down with the sole of my boot.

'Palace Purple' and lamb's-ears make a fine contrast in color and texture of foliage. An excellent trio consists of 'Palace Purple' with the silver Japanese painted fern and *Ajuga* 'Burgundy Glow'. The purple foliage also works well with the yellow and gold of hostas like 'Gold Standard' and 'Solar Flare'. It looks particularly nice along walks of stone or concrete, because the gray and the purple complement each other. Surround it with white anemones and *Geranium endressii* 'Wargrave Pink' for an early and late spring visual treat.

Heuchera micrantha
'Palace Purple'
(hu'ker-a mye-kran'tha)
ALUMROOT, CORALBELLS

Coralbells dance around the feet of a statue.

One of the many colors found in coralbells.

⟨ornament⟩

To me, a garden isn't a garden without these sprightly perennials. Long stems raise the sparse but delicate flower clusters above mottled foliage in a variety of colors. Coralbells are tough and easy, with many uses. These hybrids are all descendants of *H. sanguinea,* which is native to the southwestern U.S. and Mexico, and may also be listed as *H. × brizoides.*

Flowers come in the late spring through June for the Lower Midwest, shaped like tiny bells in white, pink, and shades of red. The blossom spikes get up to thirty inches tall, making them good cut flowers that add a light feeling to any arrangement. The foliage tops out at about eighteen inches, depending on the cultivar, spreads one foot wide, and is mottled with gray or silver splotches.

Some I've used for a long time are *H. s.* 'Chatterbox' (deep rose-pink), 'Pluie de Feu' (a good red cultivar), and 'June Bride' (a vigorous white long-bloomer). Prolong bloom by removing the spent flowers.

Heaving, the only problem associated with coralbells, comes during our wet or alternately freezing and thawing winters. With heaving, simply pushing the crowns back down in the ground will help. Planting the crown an inch below ground level and mulching is an easy precautionary solution. During wet winters the crowns can rot unless a well-drained soil is provided.

Coralbells prefer soils that aren't rich in organic matter, but drainage is necessary for this perennial to thrive. They do best in full sun but will tolerate half shade.

Heucheras look good along the front and edges of larger plantings, but I think they are prettiest when planted in abundant masses by themselves, or in large numbers interspersed with other perennials.

The silvery foliage is striking as a base around lead or cast concrete ornamental pools and statuary, the grays blending to connect both with the other elements of the garden. When the flowers rise up around the ornament, it creates a worthy focal point.

When the blossoms are up on their slender stems they can lighten the heavy foliage of hosta, ferns, brunnera, and hellebores. One of my favorite ways to use coralbells is to pair them with *Pulmonaria saccharata* 'Sissinghurst White', the leaves providing a contrast in shape, and the silver markings of each blending together.

⟨ornament⟩

Heuchera sanguinea
(hu'ker-a san-gwin'e-a)
CORALBELLS

*Yellow-green H. 'August Moon', next to an urn
planted with magenta annual verbena.*

The unrivaled Hosta *'Regal Splendor'.*

In our grandmothers' time, hostas were called plantain lilies or funkia, and only a few varieties were available. There are now so many to choose from, all different in size, leaf color, shape, and texture, that it can be mind-boggling to select a few plants from a specialist nursery or catalog.

Hosta flowers—usually lavender, occasionally white—are like miniature trumpet lilies, held on straight, strong stalks. Four of my favorites have fragrant white flowers, green leaves, and are sun tolerant: *H. plantaginea* (the old-fashioned August lily), its double-flowered form, 'Aphrodite', and 'Royal Standard' (all large); and the medium 'Honeybells'.

But the colorful leaves are what make hostas unique and popular. In addition to solid colors, they can be had with contrasting leaf margins or variegations in about every combination of green, blue, gold, yellow, and even cream or white.

They come in sizes to fit every garden, from miniatures to giants six feet or more in diameter. Once mature, the majority spread in precise circles with neat, rounded tops, but there are some exceptions that are taller, like elegant vases—the frosty blue 'Krossa Regal' and its descendant, the ivory-bordered 'Regal Splendor', being two of the best.

Hostas make an excellent ground cover for half to full shade. They can take sunny positions if kept moist, but retain their colors better in more shade. (In general, the greens and golds can take more sun than the blues.) Massed, they can smother weeds. They brighten dark areas under trees, especially if variegated ones are used. They are not fussy about soil. Once in place, they can be left alone for decades. On the other hand, they do not mind being shifted about.

Years ago I did a pleasant shade garden that is still going strong. It's planted with daffodils, brunnera, and *H.* 'Royal Standard'. After the former two put on their early spring show, the hostas emerge to cover and obscure the daffodil foliage. Later, their own white blossoms are refreshing in the heat of summer.

A single specimen hosta can be placed with other perennials, such as a colony of ferns, for contrast. Or a number of hosta varieties in green, cream, and gold combinations can be woven through the ferns for wonderful effects. Hostas are perhaps at their best with ferns. The more substantial hostas anchor the planting, while the fern fronds reach up to dance in the air.

Hosta
(hos'ta)
PLANTAIN LILY

Blue foliage and yellow blossoms of St. John's wort.

Even when not in bloom, hypericum's blue foliage can add contrast to an otherwise green-dominated landscape.

122

This native is a surprisingly rugged perennial. Its blue-green foliage and spherical habit of growth are handsome, and it grows contentedly in dry, poor soils.

Bright yellow flowers two inches or more in diameter shine as if illuminated from within. Five petals ring a dense circle of slightly darker stamens, sticking up by the hundreds, like bristles on a large, flat, round brush. In the close-up photograph, taken in July, the many-bristled center is seen along with the flower in various bud stages.

The foliage is densely held in a tidy, round fashion, and the blue-green leaves are attractive. The whole plant gets about three feet tall, capable of standing with larger shrubs if desired. In fact, it looks best with dark green shrubs nearby. The stems are rich, dark brown, and maintain the round structure during the winter months.

The blue foliage and the yellow flowers give *H. frondosum* a commanding appearance in the garden or landscape. St. John's wort is handsome enough to use in positions of high visibility where conditions are favorable.

Soil doesn't have to be wonderful for *H. frondosum* to do well. They will perform in poor soils under dry conditions, in full sun or half shade. The illustration reveals a row of them growing under the shade of a *Cercis canadensis* 'Alba', in barren clay soil along a front walk. Along with the boxwood, the St. John's worts help to create an interesting entrance for this front walk.

If three feet is too tall for a shrub in a hot, dry area, this perennial will take to pruning readily. I usually have it trimmed a couple of inches after it flowers to keep it as thick as possible.

Another useful St. John's wort is *H. calycinum*, especially if a shorter hypericum is needed. Being only eighteen inches tall, this creeper makes a good ground cover for dry, shady locations. The leaves are greener in color but the flowers are the same as *H. frondosum*'s. One plant can spread two feet wide, making it economical to cover large areas.

Try either one for difficult dry shady areas, and for a perennial with bright yellow blossoms that is easy to care for.

Hypericum frondosum
(hi-per'i-kum fron-do'sum)
ST. JOHN'S WORT

Petals within petals. This variety of candytuft is called 'Snowflake'.

Candytuft used well beneath boxwood.

A very hardy and prolific-blooming perennial that flowers in the spring and keeps its rich, dark green foliage throughout the entire season. Flowers smother the foliage completely when in full bloom.

At its peak the bloom of *Iberis sempervirens* appears like brilliant white, round clouds. Each flower is held in a cluster on a single stem, from four inches tall with 'Nana' to six inches tall with 'Little Gem', and up to twelve inches with the species, *sempervirens.* Cut the branches back after the flowers finish blooming to keep the plant dense and compact. Blossoms come in early May, pouring forth an abundance of pure white flowers in varieties like 'Autumn Snow' and 'Snowflake'.

The foliage is labeled evergreen (a catch-all term used in these parts to describe any plant that retains even a minute amount of chlorophyll), but, like the Christmas fern, shouldn't be counted on to look wonderful all year. Plants spread about two feet wide, forming compact mounds.

Full sun and well-drained soil are the best situation for *Iberis sempervirens.* Well-drained soil is most important, especially in areas where there is little snow cover. Candytuft is one of those perennials that tend to rot if moisture is held around their crowns for prolonged periods.

Candytuft can look rather ragged after one of our winters because the foliage is usually exposed to the hot winter sun without any protection. This is a good time to cut it back. Cutting back is also necessary after flowering and periodically during the life of some cultivars to keep them from getting open and sprawling. Don't hesitate to chop any of them back if they become open and unruly. They take well to pruning and will be the better for it.

This short plant is best used at the front of a plant grouping. Some of the taller varieties could be used in the middle. Or plant them around the base of conifers; their green is an ideal background for the white blossoms.

I alternate candytuft with either red or yellow epimedium at the front of plantings for a variation in foliage color and texture. To get larger clumps for deeper borders, plant three together in a triangle. Candytuft is a pleasant sight hanging out over walks and walls, its fine foliage and white blossoms adding a soothing ambience to the scene.

Iberis sempervirens
(eye-ber'is sem-per-vi'renz)
CANDYTUFT

One of the many George Slade hybrids, iris 'Country Classic' with peony 'Tokio'.

Bearded iris 'Judge Mac' stands out with its violet-blue brilliance among a bed of peonies and other iris.

Iris germanica hybrids rival those of daylily, with similar astounding numbers. The abundant flowers seem to cover the entire color spectrum. According to Steven Still's *Manual of Herbaceous Ornamental Plants,* they have been hybridized to the point that the old species name, *germanica,* is inappropriate, and one should simply call them *Iris* hybrids.

It's an ancient perennial, probably the first civilized iris. Perhaps you have some decades-old bearded iris, given to you by an aunt or grandmother, that bloom regardless of neglect in late May or June. Some of the oldest wore a mix of brown and purple. All have little fuzzy tongues called beards. In general, these old iris are more resistant to borers.

Some of my favorite modern irises come from nearby Cynthiana, Kentucky, where they are raised and hybridized by George Slade. He has developed some of the best blues I've ever seen. I tend to like the solid-color shades; I blend them together with other solid colors to visually arrange a different hue.

For easy care, a strong stem is an important characteristic to keep in mind when buying an iris. All of Slade's hybrids that I have used are on strong stems, allowing them to stand upright, holding their heavy load of blossoms after a rain without much support. Leaves are grayish-green, shaped like long swords spreading out like fans as they grow, their vertical texture appealing.

Iris are tough and vigorous, but direct sun and well-drained soil are necessary for them to perform at their best. With these two criteria met, bearded iris adapt well to different soils if helped a bit by adding organic matter at planting time.

Their large rhizomatous roots are usually planted at a slight angle, the higher end being where the leaves are present, and at least one-third of the top surface above ground. This allows water to drain away from the roots and prevents rotting. Keep mulch off the rhizomes: it too will cause decay to set in.

Bearded iris are susceptible to a nasty little borer that can devour roots and foliage. At the first sign of these insects' tunnels in the foliage, cut the infected parts off and discard them, but not in the compost pile. Dig and dispose of infected rhizomes, and make sure all old foliage is removed from the area over winter, since it is home for the borer.

One of my favorite ways to use German iris is in beds with peonies, the peonies taking up the rear with the iris in front, standing down the taller bushes of peony and hiding the bare lower branches, mix iris with peonies and daylilies, alternating them along a sunny drive or walk, for the most carefree trio in the perennial world.

ଚ୬

Iris germanica
(eye'ris ger-man'i-ca)
BEARDED IRIS,
GERMAN IRIS

Yellow flag in a soggy spot along a front walk.

An iris for the water or wet places:
pseudacorus *or yellow flag.*

128

If you are designing for a wet, soggy area, *Iris pseudacorus* could be the answer to your problems. It is ideal for low spots in the landscape where there is a confluence of water drainage and collection. It can grow happily in water without ever being divided, and is one of the prettiest yellow irises there is. Blooming on three-foot-tall stalks, yellow flag deserves a prominent spot in the garden, its four-inch blossoms laced with brown markings and veins in May and June.

The foliage is abundant after the first season—one-inch wide, green spears slicing three to five feet upward into the air. These spears stand erect, looking wonderful all season, a strong vertical presence for the garden.

One of the most vigorous perennials, once established, *I. pseudacorus* will spread while standing in twelve inches of water. Yellow flag doesn't mind full sun when it has its feet in water or a moist site. Where it is planted with other perennials in a drier place, it will tolerate half shade. With our hot summers, this is a versatile perennial.

I've placed *pseudacorus* directly in mucky clay soils and had success, as can be seen in the accompanying photograph. I came to use the iris in this particular spot after discovering that the soil was accumulating and holding water after a ferocious downpour. I realized that I had to change the way I was thinking about planting in this area.

Another useful place I've found for pseudacorus is in the drain area of house gutters. The tall foliage will hide part of the lower gutter with its green spears, add interest all season, provide color for a month, and absorb runoff water that might otherwise get into the basement. This could work out better than calling Be-Dry Basement Company. Well, not as a substitute, but as a partial solution—a natural one, and definitely prettier.

There is a more colorful yellow flag, with yellow and green foliage in the spring: *I. p.* 'Variegata'. Its new leaves have light yellow streaks through them when they first come up. By summer, they turn green like the other *pseudacorus.*

If you have a real pond or creek, yellow flag is good to plant along the bank or even right in the water. For smaller pools, these irises can be placed in containers so they don't grow to overwhelming proportions.

Sharing the creekside or the edge of a pool could be such companions as *Iris sibirica,* graceful cattail (*Typha angustifolia*), royal fern, hosta, and astilbes. Yellow flag's size makes it prominent in a mixed planting with either shrubs or perennials. Sunken in a round planter and ringed with taxus or boxwood, for example, it would make a worthy focal point as the center axis of a garden.

Iris pseudacorus
(eye'ris sued-ak-or'us)
YELLOW FLAG

An heirloom Siberian iris, the name long lost.

White and blue Siberians with some Saunders peonies.

Not only one of the best plants for the Lower Midwest, but one of the great perennials of the world, *Iris sibirica* is adaptable to a variety of situations and therefore can be used in many ways. It is tough and virtually carefree.

Siberian iris blooms aren't as large as those of German iris, but these plants make up for it by being more versatile, more delicate-looking, and easier to care for. They bloom for about a month in shades of white to purple, including some good blues like 'Sky Wings', dark violet like the popular 'Caesar's Brother', and 'Snow Queen', a good white. Most are three feet tall, but there are some short ones coming onto the market, such as 'Little White', only fifteen inches, offered by White Flower Farm. Some have lower petals that are white with purple veins running through them like webbing.

The foliage is slender and green. Leaves, stable and refined, remain attractive throughout the entire season, spreading in dense clumps of two feet in a few years. These are good companions with all perennials, their grasslike presence a complement to any gathering.

Siberian irises will grow well in just about any soil available. They will put up with dry soils but do better in a moist location. I've used them in moisture-retaining clay in full sun and half shade (facing east or west), without any problems.

I use their spiky texture with peonies, hostas, astilbes, lavender, coralbells, and hardy geraniums for contrast in foliage. Siberian iris can be used well in any part of the border or plant grouping, but are most often placed in the middle or rear. I like using the blues or purples with short, round blue spruces for a serene study in form and balance.

A vast root system gives *Iris sibirica* its drought endurance, and also serves to make it a good perennial for sharp inclines. On a slope it will help prevent erosion, and its dense crown is impenetrable by weeds, making it easy to care for. I've even seen it come up through ivy without any problem.

The flowers as well as the spiky leaves are excellent in cut arrangements. Try them with roses 'Grüss an Aachen', 'Graham Thomas', or 'Heritage' for a lovely combination.

Plant golden *Lysimachia nummularia* 'Aurea' at the feet of Siberian iris 'Sky Wings' for a rich coupling of azure and gold, or use blue and purple Siberians with yellow pansies and golden-leaved hostas. For a cooling effect place them around peonies. They are effective in the garden juxtaposed with such hard elements as retaining walls or porch steps.

Iris sibirica
(eye'ris si-bir'i-ka)
SIBERIAN IRIS

Yellow archangel, blooming in the shade.

Yellow archangel makes an excellent ground cover.

I can't remember where I first encountered this plant, but I have learned that it is one of the best deciduous ground covers for our area. It covers with silver foliage even in adverse situations, thus adding color and interest to a scene. It brightens up places where other perennials wouldn't even think of growing, and has proven to be tougher than the *Lamium maculatum* it is usually mistaken for.

The flowers, although really secondary, are pretty in their own right, their buttery yellow open mouths showing twin lips covered with a helmet or hood. The effect is of a yellow, lobelia-like flower that blooms in whorls at the base of the leaves.

Lamiastrum galeobdolon 'Variegatum' has silver and green foliage, with the silver very prominent. This silvery foliage reflects the light to transform, say, an ordinary island bed between two driveways into a striking garden entrance.

Yellow archangel spreads rapidly. It is good in areas of half shade to full shade, and will do well in three to four hours of direct sun too. Archangel is an ideal runner to quickly cover an area, with a tolerance for different soil conditions. It does prefer well-drained soil, making it less suitable for clay types, but nevertheless deserves better than the "weedy and sprawling" description with which some references dismiss it. Aspersions aside, this vigorous runner performs impressively in dry, shady areas.

Yellow archangel belongs, however, where it will not compete with less vigorous plants. It needs to be alone or with carefully chosen companions or else it will dominate the planting. Keep it out of perennial borders unless you want a mess. Of course, its rampant growth habit can be turned to advantage as a ground cover. Another good situation is with one other tall perennial, in an isolated area as mentioned. It's ideal for the woodland garden and for all difficult, dry places. Don't forget to use it under trees and shrubs, or on islands in a hot driveway.

With their vertical growth, Siberian irises make perfect companions. For such an alliance, the lamiastrum is appropriate—the tall, vigorous iris can compete while being overrun. For another colorful combination, try it as a base cover for *Lythrum salicaria*.

I know of one *Lamiastrum* cultivar whose behavior is exemplary. If it's not coverage you need, try the less sprawling 'Herman's Pride'.

❧

Lamiastrum galeobdolon
'Variegatum'
(lam-i-a'strum gal-ee-ob'do-lon)
YELLOW ARCHANGEL

Lavender 'Munstead'.

Front and center: lavender 'Munstead', with iris foliage, Russian sage, and grasses behind and the darker lavender 'Hidcote' to the left.

Considered by some to be the preeminent herb for fragrance, *Lavandula angustifolia* is also worthy of a place in any garden, either alone or with other perennials. Fragrance has always been lavender's strongest asset. Its scent is used in soaps, sachets, potpourris, candles, bath oils, and many other products.

Two of the best cultivars for us are 'Hidcote' and 'Munstead', both from well-known English gardens. The flowers of lavender gather around the upper part of eighteen-inch stems in tight clusters of dark purple. 'Hidcote' has darker violet blossoms, as can be seen in the illustration, but both usually begin blooming around June.

For the gardener, the purple flowers make a nice, spiky presence in any type of plant grouping, and go well with whites, yellows, blues, and pinks. Try lavender with a white phlox like 'Mt. Fuji' and some *Malva alcea* 'Fastigiata' for a cheerful composition.

Lavender's gray foliage makes it invaluable for contrast with darker green foliage perennials. The thin, linear leaves form compact and rounded plants. This habit makes for a nice impression with perennials whose form is more vertical, like any of the iris, yucca, and the shorter grasses.

All-day, direct sun and good drainage are requirements of lavender. If grown under less hospitable conditions, it will have difficulty coming through our wet Lower Midwest winters. Well-drained and loamy soil texture can't be stressed enough for our area. Because of winter hardiness problems, I tend to plant lavender in the spring so it will have the entire season to become established.

For a traditional combination of contrast and compatibility try either 'Munstead' or 'Hidcote' with *Teucrium chamaedrys* (germander). The darker foliage of the germander with the gray of the lavender can be used in a perennial border as a side-by-side combination, or woven together into a flamboyant knot garden.

Lavender is a delightful surprise when planted next to a walk or steps so it can be brushed in passing. I've seen it used as an impressive edging along pathways, and for dramatic effect announcing entrances. Lavender looks good with all kinds of stone structures, whether they be walks or walls, paths or sculpture; its complementary blue-violet spikes of bloom are displayed at their best.

I usually plant lavender in groups of three when using it in a bed at least four to five feet deep. With more narrow spaces, one is usually sufficient to maintain proper scale if using taller plants in the rear. Then again, style is sometimes formed by throwing all rules to the wind. Whatever you do, have some lavender somewhere, and treat yourself by taking fresh spikes inside.

Lavandula angustifolia
(la-van'du-la ang-gust-i-fo'lee-a)
ENGLISH LAVENDER

The golden-yellow flowers of bigleaf goldenray.

Thick leaves provide a heavy base for Ligularia dentata *blossoms.*

These are bold plants whose foliage is as dramatic as their flowers. *Ligularia stenocephala* 'The Rocket' is probably the best known, but I find *L. dentata* 'Desdemona' more useful and easier to place in the garden, although it likes to stay continually moist.

With our hot summers, a location in half shade is preferable, and even then the foliage is likely to wilt. 'The Rocket' needs direct sun, making wilting a bigger problem than with 'Desdemona'. Don't let this heat intolerance deter you from using 'Desdemona'; the foliage will perk up by the next morning without any problems. To have such an interesting perennial that flourishes in a wet place is worth putting up with a bit of drooping.

'Desdemona' stands three to four feet tall on strong, reddish-purple stems, with rich yellow-orange blossoms arranged in clustered heads. The petals resemble daisy blossoms, with thin rays curving backwards from the spiny centers.

Large, leathery leaves may be twelve inches across, and the plants form impressive four-foot clumps. The leaves of 'Desdemona' unfurl the same reddish-purple as the flower stalks, turn green as they mature, but retain the rich color underneath.

Planted at a northwest corner, the 'Desdemona' in the photograph is resting in a bog-type area. This garden has a slight incline further out, resulting in water collection down where the ligularia is located. It is an ideal spot for 'Desdemona', but even here the foliage will wilt at midday.

If there isn't a wet area to deal with in your garden one can be made simply by sinking a large container (such as half a whiskey barrel) with small drainage holes into the desired spot. Alternatively, you could line the planting hole with thick, perforated plastic.

Ligularia dentata puts up with a variety of soils, but clay can provide the required situation for 'Desdemona' without any extra work—the photograph shows how well a plant can do under such circumstances.

Its liking for a wet situation makes 'Desdemona' good around water, its striking leaves the perfect foil. Another fine grouping would be with *Iris pseudacorus* and *sibirica,* hostas, and astilbes, creating visual delight beside a pond or pool.

Don't forget to use ligularia along wooded streams—another ideal situation. For me, though, its best use will remain for those problematical areas in the garden or around the house that are wet and in bright shade. I like it best with spiky companions like either of the iris mentioned above, adding a more finely textured partner, such as mint, to balance the other, bolder two.

ᐧ

Ligularia dentata
(lig-u-la'ri-a den-ta'ta)
BIGLEAF GOLDENRAY

The luscious Oriental lily 'Stargazer'.

Lily 'Casa Blanca' with purple loosestrife.

Poets have sung the praises of lilies since biblical times. They have always been celebrated for their beauty and often for their difficulty of cultivation. Luckily, many hybrids have appeared on the market since about 1925, and these are not at all difficult. You can take your pick of an amazing variety of heights and colors, but when I use lilies in a garden I usually choose shorter ones that are more stable and don't need support. I prefer the Asiatic hybrids and the Oriental hybrids because they give at least two months of bloom when planted together and provide some of the best cut flowers available. With either, large trumpet-shaped flowers stand on stems eighteen to sixty inches tall, giving you the option of a long stem for cutting or a good height for including in a group planting.

The Asiatic hybrids come in whites, pinks, yellows, reds, and oranges. 'Menton' is a popular salmon; 'Apollo' a favorite white variety. 'Connecticut King' is a glowing golden-yellow. The Asiatics bloom in June and July, and are usually unscented.

Oriental lilies are perhaps the grandest flowers ever hybridized and one of humanity's greatest achievements. The colors are rich enough to melt cataracts, and infuse life with pure joy. 'La Reve' is a sumptuous pink, 'Stargazer' a brilliant crimson with white margins, and the white 'Casa Blanca' is the epitome of purity. The Orientals are also known for the gold bands that run through the center of their petals, and for their distinctive freckles. Most have a sweet citrus fragrance, and bloom from July to August.

Although the blossoms of the Orientals are larger than those of the Asiatics, both make such an outstanding impression in the garden and as cut flowers that they should be planted together for extended bloom time and easy care.

Lilies will tolerate a variety of soils as long as water doesn't stand around the bulb. They like their heads in the sun and their feet in the shade. Four to five hours of direct light is enough to produce good blossoms for both Asiatics and Orientals as long as there is bright light for the remainder of the day.

Try lilies in groups of at least five for a stunning display. They can be used as companions with other perennials, under trees where the soil is acceptable, and underplanted with ground covers and other low-growing perennials.

If you do use lilies as cut flowers, remember that taking more than one-third of the stem will result in loss of future blossoms. Since using them effectively in an arrangement usually requires a longer stem, I recommend planting a new supply each fall, or growing some especially for cutting. The big bulb companies such as Dutch Gardens are an excellent source of healthy, inexpensive hybrid lilies.

Lilium
(lil'i-um)
LILY

Purple spikes of variegated liriope.

Lilyturf or variegated liriope, shown with yellow loosestrife.

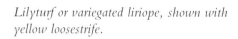

The common name aptly describes this rugged grass-like perennial in the lily family. Their dark green tufts of narrow leaves, in dense clumps, are commonly seen lining walkways to front doors, but *Liriope spicata* is versatile enough to accomplish much more.

Flower spikes of lavender, dark purple, or white are on stems about ten inches high above green or variegated foliage, depending upon the cultivar. *L. spicata* has light violet blossoms, *L. s.* 'Variegata' darker purple, and white comes from a related species, *L. muscari* 'Monroe's White'. Blossoms come at an appreciated time in late summer, usually in September.

Another popular liriope is *L. muscari* 'Majestic', used from zones 6 to 10. I've seen a white variegated form used on the island of Key West. The northern regions of the Lower Midwest should stick with cultivars of *L. spicata* for hardiness.

Lilyturf foliage is semi-evergreen and up to eighteen inches tall, the thin blades arching over. It usually turns ugly in the winter and needs a severe shearing in the spring. This can be done with a lawn mower if the lilyturf is accessible. The plants are none the worse for such a seemingly harsh practice, and it improves their appearance and saves a lot of time—especially if you have many plants.

Lilyturf will grow just about anywhere, including dry shade. I have used this perennial as a ground cover in sun to light shade. It doesn't really seem to care what kind of soil it grows in, either, doing well even in clay and compacted areas. While it does flower better in full sun, it will perform admirably in partial shade too. It is necessary to keep it away from the lawn, because it spreads by underground stems. The grass will grow into the liriope, always making it look weedy—and nearly impossible to separate!

All the cultivars mentioned above grow fast except the white one, the others spreading quickly when planted at one-foot intervals, filling an area in about three years. If I'm trying to cover a vast area with lilyturf, I economize when necessary by planting at intervals of two feet the first year and then dividing the now-established plants the third year, filling in between the first planting at one-foot intervals.

When using lilyturf along walks, I install a barrier between it and the lawn with brick, stone, or wood that goes down in the ground at least six inches. The depth is important, because it is below ground that the stems need to be inhibited.

Lilyturf is handsome in clumps of three or more in the front of a perennial border, as the third element tying trees and shrubs together to adjacent architecture, and in containers. 'Variegata' can add color as an enhancement with *Lysimachia punctata,* seen in the photograph, in front of a 'Blue Princess' holly.

The striking cardinal flower.

Cardinal flower among hostas in a shade garden.

Lobelia cardinalis is a shade-loving perennial for late summer and early fall, when its flaming color is a welcome sight. It can brighten the woodland garden at this time of year like no other.

The flower spikes stand up three to four feet, blazing like red torches. To me, the color is Chinese red, having a depth as if cinnabar had been mixed with black paint. There are white-flowering, pink, and even purple (L. × vedrariensis) cultivars, but red remains my favorite and the favorite of hummingbirds.

The foliage of most lobelias is dark, shiny green, or it can be reddish purple with L. s. 'Bee's Flame'. Some varieties have mahogany splotches on the long stems. The stalks, which are up to forty inches tall, spring from clumps of basal rosettes, each rosette sending up its own stem, one plant spreading about two feet.

Lobelia cardinalis usually blooms from July to August in half shade to full sun. L. × 'Compliment Scarlet' is one that will take full sun.

Lobelia siphilitica, the blue species, requires half shade. The flowers begin opening from the bottom of the stalk, moving upward as they mature. L. s. 'Blue Cardinal' is a good bluish-purple cultivar. Lobelia siphilitica is also valuable in the garden for its color and late blooming period of August and September. It is shorter, at two to three feet, but its blue blossoms make it very appealing. Cardinal flower and blue lobelia require moist soil that is rich in organic matter and drains fairly well.

Cardinal flower is striking when planted along a stream, in imitation of its natural setting. Although it is native to the eastern United States, neither it nor any other wildflower should be taken from the wild. It is readily available from nurseries, and once you have one, it can be divided and increased easily after flowering by separating the rosettes and replanting.

We don't all possess a stream by which to plant lobelia, but we can use it where the soil drains adequately and there is plenty of moisture. I like the taller cardinal flower in the dappled shade of woodland gardens for height relief among hostas and ferns. Here it can provide blossom at a time when little else is blooming.

L. cardinalis is a good companion for Ligularia dentata and Sedum telephium 'Atropurpureum', both sharing the burgundy coloration in the foliage, and each different in texture.

Use the blue lobelia in shadier spots for flowers in late August and September to extend the shade garden's blooming period. Try it with ferns for a cool feeling during this hot time of year.

I've had success with cardinal flower and blue lobelia in perennial groupings that are watered weekly. A naturally moist situation is ideal, but lobelias do have some tolerance out of their native habitat; so try them. Surround cardinal flower with red and white impatiens for a pleasant effect, or add some of the annual blue lobelia for an out-of-season Fourth of July celebration.

Lobelia cardinalis

(lō-be'-li-a car-di-na'lis)

CARDINAL FLOWER

The white heads of gooseneck loosestrife.

Bottom left: Gooseneck loosestrife filling in around a Foster holly.

Not a perennial to turn your back on, the most commonly known loosestrife, *Lysimachia clethroides,* can nonetheless be harnessed to serve in the garden and landscape. The gardener does need to beware of its running habit, but used with discernment it can make an effective ground cover or combine with grasses to create a beautiful meadow.

White clusters of flowers taper and crook over at the top, each shaped and bent like a goose's neck. They stand about two feet tall on thick stems with elliptical olive-green foliage. The blossoms are impressive in large masses; the bigger the planting, the more natural-looking the effect. There's no problem having large masses once you plant gooseneck; it will proliferate at a rate reminiscent of kudzu. Underground rhizomes push up a new stem every quarter of an inch—maybe more. I've seen it compete with ornamental lighting fixtures.

It is tolerant of sun and shade, clay and loam; I've not seen any light or soil condition stop it unless it was extremely dry—gooseneck does need moisture.

Instead of placing gooseneck in a perennial border, where you will have to lift a section to control it, use it to reduce your workload, and have a gaggle of charming white flowers.

Do not plant loosestrife anywhere you want to grow anything else, with the exceptions noted below. One safe situation is as a companion under and around newly planted trees and shrubs. The gooseneck can fill vacant spaces around the trees and shrubs until they fill out. Even this scenario is not without danger if precautions aren't taken to ensure that a barrier is in place between the plantings and lawn areas. As the trees and shrubs expand in size, taking over the area, the gooseneck will either be shaded out or grown over. Island placement with a proper stone or brick edging can be appropriate, as can moist sites along streams and ponds where gooseneck looks natural.

L. clethroides is good for naturalizing with bulbs and other wildflowers too. I've used it to cover the feet of daylilies successfully with a natural effect.

Perhaps best of all, plant gooseneck with larger companions in an informal-style perennial border. Lythrum, the taller grasses, Russian sage, Joe-Pye-weed (*Eupatorium* 'Gateway'), hibiscus, and other sizable and vigorous perennials would tolerate the competition. Use them all together—and send me a picture.

Lysimachia clethroides
(lye-si-mok'ee-a kleth-roy'deez)
GOOSENECK
LOOSESTRIFE

*Moneywort (*Lysimachia nummularia *'Aurea') blooming with lamb's-ears.*

A good ground cover, 'Aurea' sits well with annual lobelia.

A better or more colorful creeper cannot be found for garden use than *Lysimachia nummularia* 'Aurea'. The bright, round foliage hugs the ground and keeps a spot interesting all season.

'Aurea' has blossoms formed like a cup, with five pointed petals, facing upward in the shape of a dark yellow star, tucked under the lighter yellow foliage. With the green foliage of the species, *L. nummularia,* or the purple of *L. ciliata* 'Atropurpurea', the flowers can be seen more easily because of the contrast between flower and leaf.

The foliage of 'Aurea' provides continual interest long after the blooms of late spring and early summer have gone. Leaves are shaped like little round coins, hence one of its common names. This lysimachia doesn't encroach the way gooseneck does, but it will move around. The biggest problem with 'Aurea' is that it will get into the lawn if you have grass up to the planting edge.

It is a delightful ground cover in any sunny or shady area. The moneyworts will thrive in either situation, 'Aurea' having brighter color in the sun. None seem to be fussy about soil as long as it is moist soil.

Moneywort is a perennial to use with larger companions, such as the taller iris, peonies, or blue spruces. With oregano, campanulas, or any other short perennial it might encroach too much.

Since I first used 'Aurea' I have always wanted to plant it over blue-flowering bulbs like crocus, hyacinths, Virginia bluebells, or *Scilla sibirica.* It does wonderful things for blue. A little white wouldn't hurt either: bloodroot, or tulip 'Spring Green'.

With its yellow foliage, 'Aurea' can tie together many color combinations. Reds and oranges could be used with it for a hotter color mixture. My favorite is as a ground cover with short, round blue spruces like *Picea pungens* 'R. H. Montgomery', or *P. p.* 'Thume'. Add a hundred *Anemone* 'Blanda' for a white complement in the spring, and load the camera.

Lysimachia nummularia

(lye-si-mok'ee-a num-u-la'ri-a)

MONEYWORT,
CREEPING JENNY

Spiked whorls of the yellow loosestrife.

*Yellow loosestrife fronting African sculpture,
with variegated red-twig dogwood
behind globe spruce, right, and annual
lobelia in front.*

148

My favorite loosestrife, *Lysimachia punctata,* is an Asian species that shares the same bright yellow flowers as the previous lysimachias. Yellow loosestrife is the most versatile lysimachia, and the most useful in the garden.

The dark yellow flowers seem to float on the bed of leaves, peeking out at precise intervals on the stems. The flowers of *L. punctata* are larger than those of *L. nummularia* and *L. clethroides,* making it somewhat showier for the garden. Blossoms usually come during May and June, bursting out from the foliage and dominating the scene.

Whorled foliage gives yellow loosestrife distinction and textural interest after blooming. The mature plant usually stands about two feet on sturdy stems.

Sun or half shade is suitable for yellow loosestrife, and it can withstand our muggy summers. I've used it with success in four hours of direct sun and in full sun up to eight hours. Like the other loosestrifes, *L. punctata* likes moist soil and will spread rapidly when the soil is both fertile and moist. A drier soil in a shadier situation will slow the spreading habit.

Clay will also slow the expansion of yellow loosestrife, while at the same time providing the moisture and low fertility it enjoys. I've had *L. punctata* in a clay soil for six years without its threatening plants nearby or spreading where I didn't want it to be except into the lawn's edge. Make sure the clay doesn't allow the water to stand for days and you shouldn't have any trouble using yellow loosestrife in a clay-based soil.

If you are working with good soil and high fertility, *L. punctata* should be confined to an area where it can wantonly spread. In a clay-based soil, try it as I have with other perennials such as liriope, or along a walk where it is restricted by a path on two sides and something like a holly on the third side.

Another good combination and safe area (remember, this is in clay soil) is shown in one of the photographs, with variegated hosta and a 'Thume' blue spruce. The yellow loosestrife gets maybe four hours of direct light in the morning and bright light the rest of the day, being shaded by the branches of a variegated red-twig dogwood.

Unleashed, yellow loosestrife can be a great ground cover. This is another perennial that serves well with larger, vigorous companions it can't run over. Try it with Russian sage (the blue will be attractive with the yellow), garden phlox (tall enough to compete), and as a base cover for boltonia.

Lysimachia punctata

(lye-si-mok'ee-a punk-ta'ta)

YELLOW LOOSESTRIFE

A less invasive loosestrife is Lythrum virgatum. *'Robert' is the name of this variety.*

Purple loosestrife (Lythrum salicaria) *with an orange and yellow honeysuckle.*

This is the purple loosestrife of European origin that is responsible for choking out native plants in marshes and native meadowlands and ruining waterfowl areas. It has caused such problems that most popular catalogs have stopped offering it for sale. The named cultivars do not carry the same disfavor; nevertheless, use caution when buying and placing this perennial.

One of the best features of purple loosestrife is its long blooming period, from late June to early September. Blossom color varies from magenta to a rose pink. The blossom stalks stand three to four feet in a tight cluster of tiny flowers smothering the top foot or so. Some of the "safe" *L. salicaria* varieties are `Firecandle', with reddish flowers, `Roseum Superbum', with reddish-purple blossoms, and `The Beacon', with darker magenta.

A related species, *L. virgatum,* is preferred because it has proven to be less invasive than *L. salicaria.* The cultivars of *virgatum* are usually the ones available and the ones better known: 'Morden Gleam' is a dark rose pink and about three feet tall. 'Morden Pink' offers a truer pink. 'Robert' is a lustrous pink, one of the better compact plants at two or three feet, and readily available at nurseries. 'Happy' is a shorter lythrum at eighteen inches tall, one I haven't tried yet that should prove to be valuable for its height.

The foliage is dark green and stands in dense clumps that spread to three feet wide. Even after flowering the foliage holds some interest in a group planting.

Lythrum will grow in any soil as long as it has full sun most of the day. From clay to loam I've had success; it is not particular. It is excellent for those wet areas of the yard, but care should be taken not to allow its escape to nearby streams. While it has a special fondness for wet places, lythrum can be used successfully in other parts of the garden. Our hot summers are not a problem for it.

Lythrum is substantial enough to be placed next to shrubs in a mixed border, helping with the scaling down that is usually necessary when taller shrubs and conifers are used in the back of a planting. To create a beautiful scene, plant it with coreopsis—both yellow and pink—rudbeckia, white phlox, and Russian sage. It will stand nicely behind a border with daylilies if the planting is only three feet in depth. For wet areas, use lythrum with *Iris pseudacorus, Ligularia dentata,* and *Myosotis palustris.*

Japanese beetles seem to be fond of lythrum, and some falling over after heavy rains at peak blossom time is to be expected. These are its only disadvantages in the garden. The beetles can be knocked off daily if they can't be tolerated, and the falling over isn't such a bad price to pay for such a versatile perennial. Or you can always spray for the beetles and prop up the plants before they are laden with blossoms.

Lythrum salicaria
(lith'rum sal-i-ka'ri-a)
PURPLE LOOSESTRIFE

151

The soft pink of mallow—Malva alcea 'Fastigiata'.

'Fastigiata' adding color in June.

Mallow is a good summer perennial, with handsome, contrasting foliage and continuous bloom. Because of its ability to withstand summer heat it is becoming ever more popular here.

The one-and-one-half-inch pink blossom is slightly cupped in the fashion of hollyhocks, with a white center. It is reminiscent of the blooms on those dear shrubs called rose-of-Sharon. Pink blossoms are welcome in the summer as an alternative to the hotter yellows and oranges. With blues and whites they make a soothing blend.

Even with few flowers, 'Fastigiata' stands out in a garden as it does here in the background past the *Hydrangea arborescens* 'Annabelle'. (This photograph was taken in late June, when the first blossoms appeared.)

Palmate foliage looks good all season, adding an intricate appearance to any planting. The dark green leaves are deeply cut with distinct lobes. Individual plants become three to four feet tall, and are best planted tightly with companions for support because of their loose habit.

Versatile in that it will grow in just about any soil (the plant in the photograph is in pure clay), it asks only for good drainage. 'Fastigiata' is also drought tolerant; it can be used in areas with little moisture and therefore do well in some of the more difficult or neglected parts of the garden.

'Fastigiata' is good for either full sun or half shade. This allows use in all locations but north. The spot depicted here is shaded for part of the day by a brick wall. Individual mallows are not as long-lived as some other perennials, but they self-sow freely. Once you have purchased a plant, its descendants will usually be around forever.

When 'Fastigiata' is planted as an accent by itself against any gray background such as a stone wall, the pink blossoms will shine. White companions enrich the pink flowers also. Use phlox 'Mt. Fuji' or white coneflower, or, better yet, plant mallow among a large group of white foxglove.

To soften that bright aqua blue of swimming pools try mallow with *Artemisia* × 'Powis Castle' and lamb's-ears for a delicate color expression and textural distinction.

Malva alcea 'Fastigiata'
(mal'va al-kee'uh)
MALLOW

153

The creeping forget-me-not, M. palustris,
blooming beneath Hosta ventricosa.

Forget-me-nots, Myosotis sylvatica,
dominating the border.

For years, in a favorite garden, I've watched the forget-me-nots unfold each spring, carpeting the ground, making a blue lake for daffodils and tulips to come up through. It's the greatest blue of spring, as if the sky had come to earth.

Petite light blue flowers cover the light green foliage in a soft veil, each accented with a pale yellow eye. Small branching flower stems hold the blossoms in clusters about six inches above the tufts of foliage. There is not a better blue to introduce spring. Cultivars provide white and pink varieties and darker blues. *Myosotis sylvatica* var. 'Alba' has white flowers, 'Victoria Blue' dark blue, and 'Victoria Rose' soft pink.

I like mixing the pink and white with the original light blue in shady places, especially with ferns. It was difficult to think of a forget-me-not in any color but sky-blue until I mixed some together one spring and liked what I saw. The pinks and whites increase the intensity of the blues.

The foliage spreads into neat little six-inch mounds, the elongated leaves shaped like the mouse ears from which its name is derived. Plants radiate outward into colonies, covering a hospitable area by self-dividing and seeding. Myosotis is capable of covering vast areas mostly by reseeding, this being the way it sometimes survives Lower Midwest winters. Mulching does help through the winter, but make sure to pull it off in early spring or the plants will begin to rot.

M. sylvatica is unsurpassed as a filler plant in and around shrubs, trees, and other perennials. If there is enough soil to reasonably get a hand spade in, myosotis will usually work. It can make an effective blue carpet wherever needed, is stunning with any daffodils, and enhances all other colors.

M. palustris (= *M. scorpioides*) is known as the water forget-me-not, blooming after *sylvatica* but continuing to bloom all season. It is more difficult to find and worth the search because it will handle growing in boggy places, even trailing out into the water, as Beth Chatto points out in *The Damp Garden*. The water forget-me-not runs with stems along the ground and has the same blossom, but foliage of a lighter green. The only places I've seen it listed are Springbrook Gardens in Mentor, Ohio, and Michler's Greenhouses in Lexington, Kentucky.

An ideal situation is the woodland garden of light or dappled shade; forget-me-not can also be grown in sun if plenty of moisture is available. Both forget-me-nots are shallow rooted and can tolerate different types of soil easily. I've had success in all kinds of soil including clay.

Use either one, but get some. Tim Morehouse in Cincinnati uses *M. sylvatica* in his terrace urns every year for a beautiful spring display. Everyone can have some in a pot on the terrace or balcony like this, mixing them with pansies and other annuals for a change.

Myosotis sylvatica
(mi-o-so'tis sil-va'ti-ca)
FORGET-ME-NOT

Catmint blossoms.

Catmint blooming around stones with darker salvia to the left.

I know what you're thinking: I'm not going to plant that stuff; I don't want cats wallowing around in my garden, destroying all my hard work! But never fear: although *Nepeta × faassenii* carries the common name catmint, I have yet to witness any feline attraction to this perennial. *Nepeta cataria*—cat*nip*—is the plant cats favor, eating seedlings down to a nub.

N. × faassenii's long bloom time alone is reason to recommend it. It flowers from late spring to early summer, and cutting it back after this time will result in another flush of blossom. The lavender blue flowers are spaced at intervals in tight clusters all around the stem, standing fifteen inches tall in an attractive, airy show.

N. × 'Six Hills Giant', a three-foot-tall and -wide cultivar, will supposedly put up with more humidity than the species, according to one of its purveyors, White Flower Farm. This could prove useful to those of us in the casserole of Lower Midwest summers. Another cultivar, *N. ×* 'Dropmore', has a darker blue blossom and is eighteen inches tall.

Catmint has delicate grayish-green foliage, giving the blue flowers the best of backgrounds. The foliage does more than look good in the heat, standing eight inches tall in a tidy, round formation. I used this perennial ten years ago along a scorching driveway with lots of gravel and blacktop debris, and it is still there today, looking good.

Hot, dry, and well-drained soil can be home. Catmint will tolerate undesirable sites, making it a choice perennial for unamended soil situations in full sun. When rained upon, it will sprawl, and the flower spikes will turn up to the light. If you don't like this effect and don't want to stake it, cut it back by about half after flowering.

Nepeta is nice along driveways or in linear plantings, but I like it best interrupted with other perennials or annuals. It can function in a smaller situation as a single plant—in the middle of a small herb garden, or a narrow bed.

The blue of catmint is fine with about any other color in the garden, and wonderful with white and pink for a gentle mix. It is also great with yellows of any kind. Try it as a companion for the floribunda roses 'Sun Flare' or 'Charles Austin'. I usually plant at least three together to create a solid block of color. It is often used along the front of a perennial border as an edging plant, but I don't use it this way unless there are taller perennials behind and the border is at least five feet deep.

❧

Nepeta × faassenii
(nep'e-ta fah-sen'e-eye)
CATMINT

*Decorative golden oregano with
ajuga 'Metallica Crispa'.*

*To the right, golden oregano, adding color
as well as serving as a ground cover.*

The edible landscape is made possible with perennials like oregano. Ordinary green oregano is attractive enough, but with the golden-leaved cultivar 'Aurea' the gardener has both an herb to cook with and a valuable ornamental. What could be better than visiting your garden and picking something to help with dinner?

The leaves of 'Aurea' are a brilliant golden yellow, spreading two feet. There is no mistaking where the plant is in the adjacent photograph—its foliage glows like a splash of sun.

The flowers of *Origanum vulgare,* white to pinkish purple like those of *O. v.* 'Aurea', are insignificant and are usually removed.

The species, *O. vulgare,* loves the sun, while 'Aurea' does better in half shade—an eastern-facing location is ideal. 'Aurea' needs protection from our scorching summer sun to prevent leaf burn. Together, they provide edible ground covers for different locations. Both need well-drained soil, but I have found this can be stretched with 'Aurea' even on a clay base if the top four to six inches of soil does not hold water.

Vulgare gets about two feet tall and can be cut back any time, preferably once just before flowering to promote new growth. This will keep it looking good throughout the season. 'Aurea' makes a shorter ground cover, never getting more than six inches tall for me here in Lexington.

To plant with other perennials, I prefer golden oregano. Its bright, spreading foliage can illuminate the ground beneath shrubs and around other plants. Without question, use it with a golden hosta like 'Sum and Substance' or the white-edged 'Moonlight' for a monochromatic display.

I like using the radiant 'Aurea' with every color, but blue companions are my favorites. Geranium 'Johnson's Blue' comes to mind, along with any blue hosta, say, 'Halcyon' or 'Blue Angel'. Golden oregano is heaven with early blue bulbs, such as dwarf iris or wood hyacinths, poking up through its amber cloak. As you can see in the photograph, it does not look too shabby with variegated hostas either.

For a stunning yellow garden, choose either *Berberis thunbergii* 'Aurea' or *Spiraea × bumalda* 'Lime Mound' and plant five of them in a cluster. Back this with a row of three yellow-twig dogwoods (*Cornus sericea* 'Flaviramea'), and three witch hazels (*Hamamelis mollis*) behind those. Then edge along the front of the cluster with *O.* 'Aurea'.

ᗧ

Origanum vulgare
(o-rig'a-num vul-ga'ree)
OREGANO

A bed of single peonies with bearded iris.

Peony 'Coral 'n' Gold'.

160

A midwestern garden cannot be complete without peonies. Their foliage adds luster to any border, and they are naturals for planting in masses alone. My particular favorites are the single-flowering types, not just because they stand erect better than the big doubles after a rain, but because of the way their exposed stamens complement the flower petals.

Peony blossoms come in white, pink, red, yellow, and all shades in between. From late spring to early summer, peonies can fill the garden with vibrant color and provide excellent cut flowers for bouquets. Who could pass up peonies offered by Klehm's Nursery, in South Barrington, Illinois, like the luscious 'Honey Gold', or 'Bev', a gorgeous double, rich pink in the center fading to light pink at the tips, or 'Nick Shaylor', or 'Susie Q'? Double peonies have a tendency to fall over, but usually remain an impressive sight nonetheless.

A favorite single of many gardeners is 'Krinkled White', with frilly petals giving a lacy appearance. Some other singles and semi-doubles I've been impressed with for color alone are: 'Coral 'n' Gold', 'Doreen', 'Cheddar Supreme', 'Do Tell', and 'Kukenu-Jishia', a huge light pink with rose shading on the outer petal edges.

Peonies do best in full sun, but will flower in less light (east facing, with bright light the remainder of the day). If the soil drains well peonies can tolerate less than ideal fertility and texture if they have to. I've had peonies in clay for many years, but drainage is adequate.

Once planted, they do like to be left alone—for decades if possible. But don't let their preference for permanence inhibit you from trying them. They can be moved at any time if it is done properly. Early October is the best time for our area; dig a large hole (to lift as many of the tuberous roots as possible) and place the crown no more than one or two inches below ground level. This cannot be over-emphasized, whether moving plants or setting new ones1: they will not bloom if planted any deeper. I usually plant new or transplanted peonies at ground level, allowing a few weeks for the soil to settle. If necessary, additional soil can be applied over the root crown to cover it. This method ensures that the crown is not too deep.

Peonies create an imposing presence by attaining shrub size of three to four feet tall. The only problems peonies may suffer from in our area are stem wilt and botrytis. The best remedy for stem wilt is to cut the affected stems off and dispose of them—but not in the compost pile. If botrytis fungus infects the buds, they are best cut off, but be careful to spray your pruners with alcohol between cuts to prevent spreading the disease. Overall, these diseases do not occur often enough to render the peony undeserving of its carefree label.

Paeonia
(pee-o'ni-a)
PEONY

Centered in front of the bay window for easy
viewing is a tree peony.

A lush tree peony, 'Marchioness'.

162

The irresistible tree peony has the largest and lushest blossoms you are likely to come across in a temperate-zone garden. Flowers up to eight inches in diameter are available in white, reds, yellows, and shades in between, including rose pink, coppery gold, and light to dark pinks. The blossoms are single to semi-double, usually borne alone on thick, woody branches. Part of the attraction is the wondrous stamens, in shades from cream to orange, arranged in dense clusters like sea anemones.

Check out the lush, coppery blossom of 'Marchioness' in the close-up. 'Shintenchi' is a wonderful pink semi-double from Klehm's Nursery. 'Silver Sails' is a soft lemon yellow with orange stamens, hybridized by A. P. Saunders. 'Banquet' from Saunders is a deep strawberry-red with cutleaf foliage.

The foliage of tree peonies is beautiful by itself, deeply cut like oversized oak leaves, sometimes brushed with a bluish-gray tint, sometimes gray-green, and sometimes darker green with burgundy midribs, as with 'Haku Benryu', which sports huge, semi-double white blossoms. Bushes can spread four feet and get about four feet tall. The foliage always looks good, providing excellent texture and structure for visual interest throughout the gardening season. Sometimes stem wilt occurs on tree peonies. Use the same precautions suggested for herbaceous peonies described earlier. They must never be cut down after flowering.

Full sun or half shade will satisfy the needs of tree peonies. The one pictured here faces northeast and flowers some each year, although it gets only about three hours of direct morning light each day. Moving it around to the east side would undoubtedly result in more blooms, but then the blossoms could not be viewed from the bay window—a consideration when planning.

The major factor with these deep-rooted plants is well-drained soil. Deep, fertile soil is second. I have had success with tree peonies in some clay soils as long as water isn't retained and a top dressing of fertilizer is applied in early spring (before foliage appears), and again after flowering. Tree peonies are good in prime locations for visual interest, with perennial companions like *Brunnera macrophylla* or white spring anemones planted underneath. They have a strong presence owing to their size and can stand alone, complementing architectural features or blocking unsightly foundations.

Planted in a mixed border with shrubs and other perennials, tree peonies are ideal transition plants. It is only fair to warn you, though, that once you see their first exotic blossoms a collection of tree peonies may be in your future, and Gardeners Anonymous not far behind.

Paeonia suffruticosa
(pee-o'ni-a su-fru-ti-co'sa)
TREE PEONY

A pink Oriental poppy holds the back of this planting.
In front, l. to r., are valerian, annual nigella, hardy
geraniums, and petunias.

Oriental poppy.

Poppies are the electric lights of the perennial border. Their flowers are so bright they can't be overlooked in the garden. Although not especially vigorous, they are certainly one of the most popular flowers in American gardens. The bright orange one with a cluster of black stamens in the center has been planted in the Lower Midwest for longer than the oldest gardeners can remember.

There is a vast selection of Oriental poppies to choose from, with colors ranging from white and shades of pink to the darkest of reds. The flowers are four to six inches across and are best kept out of windy areas because of their fragility. Choose pastel shades in gardens with a softer color scheme, or use the fiery reds and oranges for a bolder effect. Bloom time is usually late May through June. One of the long-time favorites is 'Mrs. Perry', a creamy salmon-pink with an apricot tint.

The foliage of Oriental poppies is thistle-like, deeply cut and serrated, and usually twelve inches long. The leaves add an interesting texture while they are around. The foliage eventually disappears, though, so it is necessary to plant a perennial such as Russian sage nearby to cover the bare spot.

Oriental poppies need full sun or half shade, such as three to four hours of direct light, then shade for the rest of the day. They will survive our winters only if they have perfect drainage. Wet crowns will deteriorate rapidly without mulch to help during winter. I use only pine bark mini-nuggets for this purpose. The shredded types are too dense, compacting too much, and the coarser pine bark chips are cumbersome and awkward to work in the rest of the year.

The most important thing to remember about using poppies in the garden is to plant a companion that will hide the deteriorating foliage and the vacant space when the poppies go dormant. I tend to plant them alone if they are to be used as cut flowers, or with complementary (opposite) colors to tone down their dominating character.

Papaver orientale
(pa-pah'ver o-ree-en-ta'lee)
ORIENTAL POPPY

A living bouquet of Russian sage with the grapeleaf anemone 'Robustissima'.

Russian sage emerging through Hydrangea paniculata 'Grandiflora', left, with a golden spirea on the right.

As gardeners experiment with different perennials over the years, they occasionally encounter one so impressive that they wonder how they got along without it. *Perovskia atriplicifolia* is certainly such a gem, with its clouds of spiky blue flowers dancing on whitish foliage. Its delicate appearance makes it a good companion for almost all other perennials, while its size renders it appropriate with shrubs.

Small lavender blue flowers spaced around the stem at intervals form long spikes, which rise to four feet tall on upright branches. Bloom begins around late June and continues all summer, with sporadic flowering continuing until frost.

After the flowers finally close down their show the foliage takes over, holding some color, form, and texture through the winter. In early spring it should be cut down to encourage strong new growth for the coming season. Plants get four feet wide, branching out from the base like candelabras, full but delicate because of the finely cut leaves resembling miniature dusty miller foliage.

Full sun is required for Russian sage to do its best. It will tolerate a variety of soils if it has good drainage. The Russian sage in the accompanying photographs is growing in a clay soil.

Perovskia will add grace to any garden, especially with shrubs. If you broaden your definition of "perennials" to encompass shrubs and trees (which, after all, they are), and think of using all of them together, the garden will be the better for it. Thinking of them all as one provides harmony and continuity.

Placed in an island of shrubs and backed with American hollies, Russian sage can be nestled between *Hydrangea paniculata* 'Grandiflora' and *Spiraea × bumalda* 'Goldflame', adding the magical third element that turns a merely good arrangement into a truly stylish one.

P. a. 'Blue Spire' is shown in the close-up with a pink grapeleaf anemone, 'Robustissima', in September. Russian sage goes well with most perennial colors—pink, yellow, and white being my favorites. Try it with rudbeckia and various sedums for a fall display, edged with lamb's-ears to join them all together.

Russian sage is substantial enough to use behind shorter perennials in smaller, narrower borders. On the other hand, I can think of no better perennial to plant in large quantities for a carefree display all season long.

Perovskia atriplicifolia
(pe-rof'ski-a a-tri-pli-ki-fo'lee-a)
RUSSIAN SAGE

Pinwheels of woodland phlox.

*Woodland phlox in a shade garden with
hardy geranium to the rear and
European ginger in front.*

One of the prettiest lavender-blue flowers for the shade garden, and—since the native habitat is a woodland setting—one of the best ground covers available for shady areas, this native species blooms from late spring to early summer. Tight, spiraling buds unfold to become precise, five-petaled blossoms with notched edges. Flower stems get about twelve inches tall with blossoms clustering on the top portion, densely covering the foliage below. 'Chattahoochee' is a lavender-blue variety with a dark purple eye and a relatively long blooming period. There is a good white cultivar named 'Fuller's White', and a darker blue one, *P. var. laphamii.*

Dark green foliage stands erect with lance-shaped opposite leaves in exact formation. After flowering the leaves make a neat mat of glossy foliage for interesting texture the rest of the season.

Half to full shade is required for woodland phlox. Dappled shade through deciduous trees and an eastern-facing location are ideal. Moist, humus soil is best, but *divaricata*'s shallow roots allow it to adapt to clay if there is some organic matter in the top four inches of soil.

Shade-tolerant perennials this good are not numerous, and woodland phlox is a jewel among them. It is at home with companions of hostas, ferns, and other shade-loving plants. It can be a filler between perennials and a ground cover that can tie the floor of the planting to the other vertical elements.

As a ground cover under high-limbed trees with rhododendrons or *Hydrangea quercifoila,* woodland phlox with its blanket of blue blossoms can provide a wonderful cooling effect. I like to use it in an eastern location with gold hostas for contrast or with blue hostas for a monochromatic scheme. The white variety 'Fuller's White' can enhance the "cool" look when used with either gold or blue hostas.

The first time I saw *Phlox divaricata* it was being grown in the front of a typical perennial border as an edging plant. Phlox will spread outward about twelve inches, making a showy clump in the front of a perennial planting.

When using woodland phlox as a ground cover try planting the new plants in the spring on one-foot centers, and allow them to grow all year. They should have doubled in size by the next spring. You can then divide each clump in half to thicken the planting.

Phlox divaricata
(floks di-var-i-ka'ta)
WOODLAND PHLOX,
WILD SWEET WILLIAM

Garden phlox along a wall.

Garden phlox 'Mt. Fuji'.

An indispensable perennial for summer, *Phlox paniculata* varieties bloom into the fall. They are vigorous and reliable year after year.

Twelve-inch clusters of individual flowers make up a round-topped cone in white, pink, lilac, purple, or red. One of the tallest garden phlox, 'Dresden China', tops out at four feet, and happens to be one of my favorite colors, a shell pink with a deeper pink eye. Springbrook Gardens, located in Mentor, Ohio, carries varieties I have used since the mid-seventies. Thirty-inch 'Charles Curtis' is a wonderful sunset red; another pink favorite, 'Dodo Hanbury Forbes', has a solid pink blossom head. Spent flower heads should be faithfully removed to prevent germination of inferior seedlings and to extend flowering.

The foliage spreads in dense clumps with lush green leaves on strong, erect stems. Powdery mildew can disfigure phlox foliage, but damage is minimized if you water from the bottom and space the plants so that air can circulate on all sides.

Two garden phlox that are less susceptible to powdery mildew are 'Mt. Fuji' (or 'Fujiyama') and *P. carolina* 'Miss Lingard'. These two whites do best in our humid Lower Midwest summers, and seem to be more vigorous. 'Miss Lingard' begins to flower in June and can be planted with the later-blossoming 'Mt. Fuji' to provide a succession of white blossoms for several months. 'Mt. Fuji' has some of the biggest flower heads at fifteen inches, and is highly recommended.

Full sun discourages powdery mildew, but phlox will also accept half shade. The best soil is well drained and rich in humus and nutrients. If the soil is not fertile, phlox can benefit from a weekly watering and a monthly fertilizer application during the growth period.

Garden phlox can stand with other tall perennials such as Russian sage, lythrum, and peonies. With daylilies and iris they make a carefree combination. The taller varieties can be placed in front of shrubs to scale down a planting and bring cool relief to the green.

Choose the colors you like best, and don't refuse the old purple variety if a neighbor offers you some. It looks great planted in front of *Hibiscus syriacus* 'Bluebird' with annual pink and white *Cleome spinosa* in between. As an added bonus, hummingbirds are attracted to both phlox and cleome.

Phlox paniculata
(floks pan-ik'u-la'ta)
GARDEN PHLOX

Blue balloon flower.

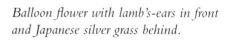

Balloon flower with lamb's-ears in front and Japanese silver grass behind.

When I write of *Platycodon grandiflorus* I am thinking primarily of the blue ones. The blues have always been successful for me, and are definitely the showiest. I admit that I cannot say enough about the effectiveness of blue in a garden.

Balloon flower is unique when in bud stage, well described by its common name. There are single and double types. The stamens and pistils in the centers of the blue ones are more defined, forming a distinct star pattern. The blues are violet-blue, rich and refreshing to see blooming in summer, usually from June to July, and sporadically all the way to September. Their value as cut flowers is reason enough to have some. Flowers are two to three inches wide, shaped like broad bells peeled back with five pointed sections.

There are other colors of balloon flower. White and pink come in 'Fuji Mix', up to sixteen inches tall. Some of these shorter ones like 'Fuji' are better used in the perennial border, mainly because they stand on their own without support (which means less work for the gardener).

Wayside Gardens has a good double blue balloon flower that tops out at eighteen inches, appropriately called 'Double Blue'. The flowers on this one resemble those in the photograph, but are shorter. There is an eight- to ten-inch violet-blue, 'Apoyama', purported to bloom all summer, that can be found through Busse Gardens in Minnesota. White Flower Farm is offering a new fifteen-inch dwarf called 'Sentimental Blue' (some catalogs label it shorter, but I recommend trying it for yourself), with single blossoms, suitable for the border or for cutting.

The leaves are thick and dark green, shaped like fat lances with toothed edges—good enough for holding the expressive bell blossoms.

Platycodon can tolerate full sun to half shade, with the taller ones, I think, better off in direct sun. Soil should drain well and not retain moisture for a long period. Allow balloon flower plenty of time to come up in the spring; it is a slow starter.

The blue balloon flower looks best with white around it in some form. *Stachys byzantina* fronts the three-tiered combination in the photograph, with Japanese silver grass in the back. Mix it with blue's complementary color, yellow, in the form of *Lysimachia nummularia* 'Aurea', along with some pink phlox 'Dresden China', for a softer effect.

I use the taller balloon flowers in the blue form as a cut flower; their height is worth the extra attention they require for cutting purposes. Try the shorter mixture of all three colors in a planting with grass—blue fescue and variegated liriope.

But if you try only one, make it blue.

Platycodon grandiflorus
(plat-i-ko'don gran-di-flo'rus)
BALLOON FLOWER

The distinctive variegated Solomon's seal on the right, with jack-in-the-pulpit foliage, bottom, and brunnera.

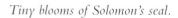

Tiny blooms of Solomon's seal.

I have nothing against our native Solomon's seal, *Polygonatum biflorum*. It is a carefree ground cover in the shadiest parts of a border, in woodland settings, and under trees, attaining a height of about three feet. In the same situations, the non-native but more decorative *P. odoratum* 'Variegatum', with its white variegation, also adds a bright relief from the monotony of green.

The blossoms—tiny, elongated bells—begin in May for the Lower Midwest. Dangling in twos or threes, they hang from the lower part of the stem at regular intervals like well-spaced garments on a clothesline. They are usually ivory, often with a tinge of green, and sweetly scented. Fall brings dark blue berries that add a nice contrast to the variegated foliage, dangling down as the flowers did.

The stems arch over gracefully, lifting the leaves on the top side of the stem like little wings riding an updraft. Cream-variegated leaves alternate on the upper surface of dark brown, two-foot stems. The variegated foliage has a warm effect in the shade garden, glimmering in soft light, and also enhances cut-flower arrangements.

In light to deep shade, given moist soil and a cool environment, the plants will spread rapidly. I place Solomon's seal in the shade garden and allow it to naturalize among the other shade perennials. This is what it is going to do anyway. If the gardener does not want it in a particular spot—say, crowding a cherished hosta—it is easy enough to pull out. I like to use 'Variegatum' with hostas 'Francee' and 'Undulata Albo-marginata', the white and green of them all creating an impressive combination.

Solomon seal's foliage offers good contrast in texture and color when interspersed with fern colonies. Try it in front of tall glade ferns, or rising above Christmas ferns.

Where you find Solomon's seal in its natural habitat, you also usually find Jacob's ladder and the native bleeding-hearts called Dutchman's breeches and squirrel corn. To this mix add a few violets and larkspur and you will have the perfect illustration of what companions work well with polygonatums.

> ᘜ
> *Polygonatum odoratum*
> *'Variegatum'*
> (po-lig-o-nay'tum o-do-rah'tum)
> VARIEGATED
> SOLOMON'S SEAL

'Miss Willmott' on the right, under a Sargent crab.

Cinquefoil 'Miss Willmott'
against a blue spruce.

At first sight these resemble giant strawberry plants, although they produce no edible fruit. But they are hardy and tough perennials. *Potentilla fruticosa* is a shrub-type cinquefoil, usually with yellow or white blossoms, and useful in the landscape, but much taller than *P. n.* 'Miss Willmott' and 'Roxana', the perennials with which we are concerned.

The twelve-inch 'Miss Willmott' and the fifteen-inch 'Roxana' have cherry-pink and rose-orange blossoms respectively. Both spread to become wider than they are tall. 'Miss Willmott' throws branching stems with flower heads sprawling into nearby plants or nearby shrubs. Actually, they are better placed close to companions—ideally blue ones, as shown here—for this kind of support.

Blossoms of 'Miss Willmott' look like five hearts held together at the center by the pointed ends. The five petals have deep red veins, a center with the same dark red, and black stamens. There is also a dwarf *Potentilla fruticosa* called 'Sunset', a fiery red-orange, which appears promising, although I have not tried it. Wayside Gardens offers another dwarf, the only yellow potentilla that has tempted me—the three-inch *P. neumannia* 'Nana'. 'Miss Willmott' is my favorite, because it is only twelve inches tall, makes a neater-mounding plant than most cinquefoils, and carries attractive foliage through the season.

Cinquefoils are best placed where they will receive full sun in well-drained soil. They don't mind light shade, and I think in our hot summers are best given some in the heat of the day. The depicted planting of 'Miss Willmott' receives about five hours of full sun. Our intense summer heat will sometimes encourage spider mites to disfigure the leaves, but cutting the foliage down (which is advisable after flowering anyway) will generate fresh growth.

In the photo, 'Miss Willmott' is growing under a young Sargent crab, where it gets some shade. The area has a six-inch layer of topsoil but underneath is yellow clay, and you can see that "Miss W" tolerates the situation quite nicely. This is partly because the position is on a slight rise, which will always be conducive to better drainage.

If cinquefoil is used in a perennial planting it is best to have companions close by for support. Shrubs can serve the same purpose. In fact, I like them best as a partial ground cover with trees and shrubs, blended with associated colors. *Picea pungens* (blue spruce) 'Montgomery' is used here. Unseen on the other side is a yellow spirea, and white sweet alyssum laces in between.

Potentilla nepalensis
(po-ten-til'uh ne-pa-len'sis)
CINQUEFOIL

The glowing yellow coneflower or
black-eyed Susan.

Yellow coneflower highlights this
combination with Queen Anne's lace
and aster 'Monch'.

178

One of the toughest and best perennials for the Lower Midwest, *Rudbeckia fulgida,* thought coarse by some, is a beautiful yellow workhorse in the garden, vigorous and virtually indestructible. It is often called black-eyed Susan, or just rudbeckia.

Bright yellow blossoms three to four inches wide fill the garden from the middle of summer until fall. Rudbeckia is shaped like a daisy, with yellow rays surrounding a dark blackish-brown pincushion center. Besides blooming for an extended period, each flower lasts a long time. After the rays fade and fall the cone center remains on the top of the stem for added interest. Both the flowers and the cone heads are good to cut for arrangements.

The old reliable *R. f.* 'Goldsturm' is the mainstay of the garden. It is a perfect height for most situations, between eighteen and twenty-four inches. If you really want a stretch in height try another native, *R. maximum,* a seven-foot giant with gray-blue foliage. Plants of a relative, *R. hirta* 'Double Gold' (offered by Burpee), get up to three feet tall. 'Indian Summer', new from Park's, is said to offer blossoms six to nine inches across, and if it's true will be a great addition to the family.

Rudbeckias usually spread about two feet at maturity, forming dense crowns as they grow outward from the center. The leaves are coarse in texture, being hairy and dark green. I usually place several plants together for a strong display.

Being a native, yellow coneflower is appropriate for establishing in meadow gardens and prairie-type plantings. I like it in the border with Russian sage, underplanted with bulbs like tulips and lilies, and planted in large masses in front of shrubs. It is a good companion for lythrum, boltonia, phlox, and sedum.

Plant rudbeckia in front of peonies and daylilies to flower after they have had their blooming period. This is a late summer and early fall guaranteed bloomer. To soften its coarse texture and cool down the bright yellow, I like to plant it with some perennials with finer foliage such as *Artemisia×* 'Powis Castle', lavender, or white Japanese anemone.

An eastern-facing location is enough to satisfy yellow coneflower's light requirements. It will take anything from full sun to medium shade. One of the best things about coneflower is its tolerance of our hot and dry summers. I have placed it in any soil available, including clay, with successful results. In fact, it can be used just about anywhere.

Rudbeckia fulgida
(rud-bek'ee-a ful'ji-da)
YELLOW CONEFLOWER

Salvia *'East Friesland'*.

Dark purple Salvia × superba.

With its brilliant bluish-purple spikes of flowers, *Salvia × superba* has proven itself as a most reliable perennial. It blooms for a surprisingly long time, and even more bloom can be encouraged by removing the spent blossom spikes.

The flowers are blue-violet, single-lipped and hooded little open mouths, clustered all around the stem facing outward, the spikes usually four to six inches long. Perennial salvia is good to have with other lighter blues, like catmint, that bloom at the same time; the lighter color seems to increase the intensity of the darker salvia. At their best, they offer blossoms beginning in May and lasting till August.

S. s. 'Ostfriesland' (or 'East Friesland') has long been a favorite because it is only eighteen inches tall and requires no staking. 'May Night' is slightly taller. Both make our best-perennials list because they are hardy to zone 5 and can stand our humid, drought-prone summers. They also are untroubled by insects or diseases.

The stems develop a slight grayish tint as they mature, with mahogany splotches that match the lower part of the flower buds. Leaves have a seersucker-like texture. The margin has a round indentation on the entire edge of the oblong, lance-shaped leaf.

Salvias enjoy full sun with moist and well-drained soil but as mentioned earlier will tolerate dry conditions. They are therefore good for hot spots in the border and are easily grown once established.

There are lighter blue relatives such as meadow sage, *Salvia haematodes,* a beautiful three-foot plant with large, light purple flowers that acts more like a biennial.

Plant 'Ostfriesland' or 'May Night' with *Buddleia* 'Nanho Purple' in the background; Russian sage in the middle; and *Veronica* 'Sunny Border Blue', catmint, and balloon flower all grouped in clumps in front for a grand blue garden. Since a little white will always serve to make the blues seem bluer, I usually add some white phlox or coneflower (*Echinacea purpurea* 'White Swan'), or a small amount of lamb's-ears in front.

Another useful salvia is one usually considered an herb. Commonly known as sage, *S. officinalis* 'Purpurascens' has such colorful foliage that it wins a place in perennial gardens without question. I mix it in the border as I would any other perennial. Place it with golden oregano for a patch of edible purple and yellow.

෨
Salvia × superba
(Salvia nemorosa)
(sal'vee-uh)
PERENNIAL SALVIA

The fine texture of lavender cotton.

Lavender cotton softens dark maple foliage.

Santolina chamaecyparissus (S. incana) is a fine perennial that happily takes summer heat. I use it for its crisp white foliage and tightly woven texture. It's not the best of white-foliage plants, but still is worth growing for its uniquely knotted leaves. Since its small, yellow buttonlike flowers are not the main attraction, they are usually removed to keep the foliage in top shape.

The white foliage is twice divided into tiny oblong segments, each leaf measuring one-half to one inch. Individual plants can be up to two feet tall and spread about eighteen inches. With lavender cotton, I prefer the shorter (ten-inch) *S. c.* 'Nana'. 'Nana' holds its shape better than the species, which tends to fall open, particularly if allowed to become top-heavy with blossoms.

Full sun and well-drained soil are essential for lavender cotton to thrive in our humid summers. I always plant them in the spring so they can have the entire season to settle in. This precaution, along with a little mulch, helps to assure their survival during the winter months.

Lavender cotton has long been featured as a component of knot gardens because the plants respond so favorably to shearing, looking like a piece of embroidery. The white foliage is usually woven over and under a contrasting green-foliage perennial such as germander to create a distinct pattern.

Short hedges can provide an attractive outline around a bed or planting, and santolina is ideal for this purpose. I also use them with a contrasting-foliage perennial along the front of a border, alternating clumps of three. Grouping them in this way allows the white santolina to maintain the interest when its companions are not blooming. As partners·I like 'Johnson's Blue' geranium, coralbells, asters, or candytuft. However, santolina is not limited to the front of the border, being tall enough to use in the middle as well; try lavender cotton there with coneflowers—pink and white—or Siberian iris.

> ### Santolina chamae-cyparissus
> (san-to-li'na ca-me-sip'ar-iss'us)
> LAVENDER COTTON

The fall pink of 'Autumn Joy'.

Sedum 'Autumn Joy'.

Sedums are becoming as prevalent in the fall garden scene as chrysanthemums. In my opinion, they actually offer more in the long run—even through winter if left standing—than chrysanthemums ever could. Succulent leaves lend *Sedum spectabile* (recently renamed *Hylotelephium spectabile*) an exotic appeal for Lower Midwest gardens. They resemble succulents, which are cousins to the cactus. But they are perfectly hardy, reaching as far as zone 3, a zone extending into northern North Dakota.

The flower heads of sedum can be up to six inches across, made up of individual half-inch blossoms in dense, round clusters. Several of these clusters make up the entire blossom head, which looks somewhat like broccoli. Bees and butterflies love the tiny flowers; one or the other always seems to be visiting when the plant is in bloom.

S. s. 'Brilliant' with its carmine flowers is a relief from the much-praised 'Autumn Joy', a subtle pale pink color fading to rose, then remaining through winter as rusty red. 'Carmen' has rose-pink blossoms with gray-green foliage. There is a white I have not tried, with bluish-green leaves. I think 'Variegatum' looks sickly, and have never used it. *Var.* 'Atropurpurea', with burgundy foliage and light pink flowers, is weak and tends to flop.

The foliage of sedum is thick and fleshy with a smooth toothed edge. 'Brilliant' and 'Autumn Joy' are sturdy and stand up the best, making for more carefree plants.

'Autumn Joy' richly deserves its popularity. It serves longer and is more versatile than some other perennials. But I think "broccoli" when I see more than three together, my hand reaching down for my harvesting blade, itching to cut their little heads off. That is how I like to use sedums anyway—as a relief texture among other finer foliage. Sedums and grasses are superb together. The contrast thus created has a keen balance. Also, there is the nostalgic feeling you get of stepping out into your backyard and being in a farm field of wheat and broccoli. Well-drained soil is the first requirement. If sedum has good sun or light shade it will become an eighteen-inch-tall by twelve-inch-wide mound.

I use sedum with daylilies, peonies, Siberian iris, artemisia, and lamb's-ears, among others, for textural contrast and because of its bloom time. Perhaps my favorite combination is with large blue hostas, like 'Blue Angel' and *sieboldiana* 'Elegans'. The heaviness of the hosta foliage balances the thick heads and stems of the sedum.

All kidding aside, if you were to try only one perennial for the fall it should be *Sedum* 'Autumn Joy'. You might forget all about chrysanthemums.

Sedum spectabile
(Hylotelephium spectabile)
(se'dum spek-tab'i-le)
SHOWY SEDUM

Rosettes of the creeping sedum called 'Dragon's Blood'.

Fall reds: Japanese blood grass (Imperata cylindrica 'Red Baron') in the rear and sedum 'Dragon's Blood' in the foreground.

Stonecrop is a creeping, ground-hugging plant that is very different from the larger 'Autumn Joy' in color and structure. The foliage is similarly succulent but more delicate, the leaves forming small rosettes. Pink or red flowers are held on single stems that usually have four branches supporting the cluster of star-shaped flowers. Height is usually no more than two to four inches.

One of the best, 'Dragon's Blood', has deep red foliage with a bronze cast. 'Fuldaglut' is touted as a better 'Dragon's Blood', but the name is not (Fulda is a town in western Germany, *glut* means "glow," and the name probably sounds fine to German ears). Burnham Woods Nursery in Bloomington, Indiana, offers the uniquely appealing 'Variegatum', a cultivar with creamy leaves and pink margins. The photos of 'Dragon's Blood' were taken in August—still making a good show, although blooming had begun in midsummer.

Stems of stonecrop creep over the ground, rooting at intervals as they touch. The red foliage is quite commanding when used, as I saw at Burnham Woods, with blood grass. The rosettes of leaves at the terminal ends are always a darker red than those further back, and remain so during the winter months. Stonecrop is reported to grow more vigorously in the northern regions, which should give the upper areas of the Lower Midwest better success with it.

Bright sun and well-drained soil are what this creeping sedum needs. I use it between stepping stones or at the edges of gravel walks to soften them. It's not a fast spreader for large areas but will cover smaller spaces nicely. It is especially pleasing between the steps of a limestone walk or among gray pavers.

I also recommend this sedum for stone or concrete urns; when the smart red rosettes of foliage hang over the lip of the planter, they look very distinguished. Planting it atop a stone wall will give a similar effect. If neither is available, create a miniature planting in an English-style garden trough that is raised on a pedestal for easy access.

I use stonecrop as a living mulch under other perennials in the hot sun to conserve moisture and give a natural, finished appeal. Try 'Dragon's Blood' with *Scilla siberica* planted underneath for a blue spring awakening.

Alternate stonecrop with white *Stachys byzantina* 'Silver Carpet' for a colorful front border to an all-red garden. Or plant it in front of catmint, the gray-green foliage and blue blossoms of which blend well with the red foliage of stonecrop.

Sedum spurium
(se'dum spu'ri-um)
TWO-ROW STONECROP

'Silver Carpet' lamb's-ears.

A standard juniper with lamb's-ears.

Stachys byzantina is the best white-leaved accent perennial—and the easiest to grow—the gardener can find. Its soft, woolly foliage, planted with perennials or shrubs, is a great asset to cool down any color combination.

The small pinkish-purple flowers are held up on six-inch hairy white stems. They can be lovely when they first come up but usually fall over after a rain, making a mess. Some gardeners prefer to remove the flower stalks, keeping the foliage, which is the main attraction, neater. This extra maintenance is no longer necessary with the cultivar 'Silver Carpet', which does not bloom, but in all other respects is the same wonderful *S. byzantina*.

It has the most endearing leaves you can imagine, velvety soft when rubbed between the fingers, like a cat's ear or, as the common name indicates, a lamb's ear. Leaves are four inches long, oblong shaped, and narrow at both ends. The foliage spreads into dense mats only six inches tall, making it a good ground cover for small to medium-large areas. Being white, it is the perfect foil for other plants.

Sometimes lamb's-ears rots out in hot and humid weather. Thinning out and pruning in early spring before the foliage appears can head off this problem. But if it happens, simply remove the dead foliage and thin out the center of the clumps. Well-drained soil and full sun also reduce this tendency toward center rotting while providing the optimum conditions for lamb's-ears. Kurt Bluemel has developed a larger lamb's-ears called 'Helen von Stein', with bigger leaves, that is not so susceptible to rotting out.

Lamb's-ears is effective both in the front of a planting with other perennials, and in front of shrubs, with the house, or trees. The downy white foliage stays low to the ground and softens the green foliage of companions, while causing their blossom color to seem more vivid.

Use stachys to soften walks of stone or brick, gravel or mulch. Planted at the edges of a path, the foliage will spill over and tie the walkway together with the associated side plantings. Use it as a companion to hardy geraniums, coralbells, lavender, veronica, and any other perennial that likes full sun and infertile soil. Use it with shrubs as an accent, the white and green enhancing each other. Use it at the base of vertical elements, like arbors, fenceposts, and house corners. This can dramatically wed the horizontal surface of the ground to the architectural element.

Stachys byzantina
(sta'kis bi-zan-tin'a)
LAMB'S-EARS

189

Germander in bloom.

Germander and lavender creating a knot garden.

Bright shiny green foliage with serrated edges characterizes this perennial. *Teucrium chamaedrys* is mostly used for its dark green leaves: it resembles miniature boxwood, and, depending on the winter (mild, or straight from hell), is evergreen.

The flowers have their own charm if ever allowed to bloom. If they show their faces, you will see tiny tubular blossoms, light to dark purple, with lips on top and bottom. Stamens stick out like antennae from the U-shaped upper lip, inviting visitors for pollination.

Germander plants develop into tight clumps up to eighteen inches wide and twelve inches tall. The foliage is dense and delicate due to its small size, making germander an excellent perennial for contrast and one that will hold up to shearing. Plants will remain dense in any shape desired when clipped, and will look better if pruned after flowering.

If the foliage is damaged during winter (which it can be if not protected), germander withstands cutting back to about two inches, after which it will thicken again. I prefer to let winter do what it will, then cut it back in the spring.

Well-drained soil is a must, with full sun. I have had germander thrive, when planted in five hours of direct sunlight, facing east, well enough to make a tightly woven knot garden.

This edging plant can be shaped into spheres, trimmed square for neat hedges, or allowed to grow naturally. It is a great companion for santolina. Both have tight, intricate foliage, contrasting in white and green, and both are amenable to shearing. Germander is pliable for making small standards in clay pots or containers.

T. c. 'Nanum' is a cultivar that is shorter, at six to ten inches, with rose-pink blossoms. Heronswood Nursery, Ltd., in Kingston, Washington, lists a variegated germander, *T. scorodonia* 'Crispum Marginatum', with lime-green leaves edged in cream.

I use germander predominantly for crisp little hedges to outline beds of roses, peonies, or herbs. These neat green strips delineate spaces, lending a finished appearance. Such an edging is especially effective if the planting bed and the lawn are separated by brick or stone. Germander softens the hard materials and provides a green transition that will maintain the structure of a garden year-round.

Teucrium has good foliage for contrasting with lavender, artemisias, lamb's-ears, and catmint. For a striking statement, try outlining any shape you choose with germander, then plant golden oregano inside.

ତ

Teucrium chamaedrys
(tu'kri-um kam'a-drize)
GERMANDER

Meadow rue blossoms.

To the right of the head is meadow rue.

Probably the most graceful and delicate shade perennial available for the Lower Midwest. Two I am recommending can provide much-needed height, while the third has fernlike foliage which creates good relief for all the heavier-foliage plants like hostas.

Thalictrum aquilegifolium has tufts of pinkish-purple flowers shaped like fuzzy balls set on multibranching blossom stems. There are both male and female plants, with the males usually showier. The flower stalks generally reach up to three feet, tossing around in the slightest breeze. The mauve blossoms come in late spring to early summer and look good with hostas, especially the blues and the yellows. *T. rochebrunianum* 'Lavender Mist' offers the most ornamental blossoms, having lavender-violet flowers with distinctive yellow stamens. The cultivar name is appropriate. It has the advantage of blooming in late summer, but is the tallest of the three at four to six feet. *T. minus* has yellow blossoms in a dense spray above the foliage. Usually eighteen inches tall, it offers countless possibilities for intermingling with other shade perennials, either in the front of or in the middle of a planting. Its intricate foliage is a good foil for bold hostas.

T. aquilegifolium is the columbine meadow rue, so called because the plant as a whole looks like a huge columbine, with leaves the same smooth grayish-green color, mildly brushed with a bluish tint, particularly in deep shade. Columbine meadow rue has a number of cultivars, all of them invaluable for bringing a cool presence to the shade garden. 'Album' can demand attention planted in large numbers under the canopy of dogwoods that have been limbed up about four feet for a dramatic effect, with blue hostas. 'Atropurpureum' carries bicolor flowers of lilac-rose and deep purple stamens. With the added attraction of dark purple stems, it makes the perfect companion for yellow hostas in the shade.

There is a good selection of meadow rues to use in half shade, dappled shade, or an eastern-facing location. They like moist-soil environments. The taller ones are ideal to create greater depth when planted with other shade perennials. Thalictrum can withstand more sun in the northern regions of the Lower Midwest, where summers tend to be cooler.

The columbine meadow rue has proven especially valuable for deep shade. There, it will not be as tall or as vigorous, but will nonetheless make a much-needed statement in a difficult area.

> ⟨෴⟩
>
> *Thalictrum*
> (tha-lik'trum)
> MEADOW RUE

Blossoms of thyme.

Creeping thyme spilling onto a gravel path. The taller plants in back are, at left, catnip; at right, lamb's ears. The yellow is coreopsis, the pink, annual portulaca.

One woolly, one creeper, and one common thyme categorize the selections available for the gardener. The first recommended is a tiny, hairy, prostrate type, *Thymus pseudolanuginosus*—woolly thyme. The second is *T. serpyllum,* the creeping thyme, with bright green foliage. The third, *T. vulgaris* (common thyme), is the one for herb gardens and culinary use.

Flowers are arranged as small spikes of tubular clusters in some thymes and grow straight out of the leaf axils in others. Woolly thyme has rosy-purple flowers so tiny they are easy to miss, unless you either bend down or pick some to get a closer inspection. Creeping thyme offers a showier blossom with a variety of colors. There's 'Albus' with white blossoms, 'Coccineus' with red flowers, and 'Pink Chintz' with pink blossoms. Common thyme has lilac-pink blossoms, easier to observe because they stand up to twelve inches.

Thyme foliage can be quite interesting. Related to *T. vulgaris* are two scented forms, one with yellow variegation. *T. × citriodorus* is the lemon-scented thyme, and 'Aureus' is the yellow-variegated lemon thyme. *T. v.* 'Variegatus' is a variegated form of the common thyme, and one of the more vigorous for our area.

Thymes like full sun and a porous soil for drainage, and grow well in dry, poor soils. They will tolerate some shade but grow more slowly.

I usually use thyme in hot places. Woolly thyme works well around and in between stone walks and overhanging the edges of beds. Hot driveways provide a hospitable environment for all the thymes, but the creepers especially look good growing out over walkways and drives. Try the creepers, particularly the white- and golden-variegated ones, in window boxes. Mix the white-variegated one with pink petunias for a pretty combination.

Besides looking good and providing great ground covers, all but the woolly thymes can be used for culinary purposes. Place them in any perennial border, under hosts such as lilies, and in front of shrubs in direct sun. I like to use the white-variegated thyme at the front of plantings with other short companions like *Ajuga* 'Cristata' for strong contrast in color and texture.

Perhaps you have retired to a smaller, more manageable situation, or just don't have room for a garden. Try the various thymes in containers on a sunny balcony or window ledge. A couple of sprigs of lemon thyme with roasted or grilled chicken or fish can freshen anybody's day.

Thymus
(thi'mus)
THYME

Spiderwort 'Snowcap' with golden berberis.

Spiderwort 'Bluestone' on the left, standing above the cinnamon fern.

The spiderwort I am referring to here is not the native *T. virginiana,* with its luminescent blue blossoms, but a hybrid between that and another species.

Tradescantia × andersoniana has larger flowers, one to one and a half inches in width, triangular in shape, with ripples along the margins. There are three petals in the shape of a slightly cupped triangle, pushing up yellow-tipped stamens from the center like the tracking arm on a satellite dish. Bundles of flowers emerge from wrapped green sepals suspended from burgundy stems. Blooms develop at the juncture between the stem and the grasslike leaves.

If you never have time to look at your garden in the mornings, this plant is probably not for you. Flowers usually fade and are gone by midday, but blooming continues for about a month, with a good selection of available colors. Colors run from white to rosy red. 'Snowcap' with rich white blossoms is excellent, with some of the largest flowers among the cultivars. 'Bluestone' is a good deep violet-blue, and 'Iris Pritchard' sports white blooms brushed with blue. 'Pauline' offers a nice orchid-pink blossom; 'Red Cloud' has a snappy rosy-red appearance.

Spiderwort foliage is a rich dark green, folded down the center to form a V-shaped grasslike leaf. Leaves at the top grow in a swirling pattern, and spin out the bunched blossoms in tight cascades. Individual plants spread two feet wide and fifteen inches to twenty-four inches tall, depending on the cultivar. The foliage usually expends itself by midsummer, a sure sign that the gardener should cut it completely down so it can initiate new leaves, which it obligingly will with enviable ease.

These are some of the best perennials for moist areas, and a blessing for boggy spots in the garden. Given sun or half shade, they will lend a textural contrast to larger perennials.

Spiderwort is distinctive planted with hosta or ferns in an eastern-sun location. The thin green leaves of the spiderwort provide a balance for the heavier foliage of hostas. Check out the contrast of 'Bluestone' among a colony of cinnamon ferns in the accompanying photograph.

I think spiderwort is better used in half-shade situations, such as in the woodland garden and under limbed-up trees. Their flowers are more vivid in these situations, the colors richer. Such placement gives the spiderwort its optimum opportunity to be the shade-garden asset it can be.

Whether you decide to use spiderwort in the sun or half shade, you won't be disappointed with the results. Show off the dark green foliage and white blossoms of 'Snowcap' by placing it with golden shrubs, such as *Berberis thunbergii* 'Aurea' or *Spiraea × bumalda* 'Lime Mound' for a remarkably bright spot in your garden.

ഏ

Tradescantia × andersoniana
(trad-es-kan'shi-a
an-der-son'ee-a'na)
SPIDERWORT

197

Graceful cattail.

Wet partners: graceful cattail and a
pussy willow.

This may seem an unusual plant to be recommending for the garden, but it is a very useful one for wet areas when properly controlled. It definitely has its place, along with other water-loving perennials. *Typha angustifolia* is not for average garden situations, but is unequaled for specific problems: water-retaining clay soil, or any wet areas.

Dark brown candles called catkins make up the flowers called cattails. Everybody knows what they are, and has seen them in some part of the North American continent. Graceful cattail richly deserves its name, being smaller and shorter and having thinner catkins than its roadside relative, *T. latifolia*.

Thinner catkins and foliage make graceful cattail better for various placements and situations in smaller gardens. The catkin is made up of two parts—a thicker reddish-brown tube about three feet up the stalk, and a thinner, lighter colored one at the top—as can be seen in the photographs.

Water features and associated plantings are a necessary part of a complete garden. Graceful cattail offers the polished stature and natural charm of cattail on a diminished scale, so that it can be enjoyed in even the tiniest garden.

Full sun is a must with cattails, as is constant moisture. Their favorite place is standing in water along a stream, or in a boggy area where water collects.

Caution must be taken when using graceful cattail in the garden. Some type of confinement is essential. An old whiskey barrel is ideal for this purpose. Kentucky seems to have a surplus of these items, but I've seen them in other parts of the Lower Midwest too. If a whiskey barrel is not available, something like a muck bucket (a large-diameter, two-handled, heavy plastic container available at farm-supply and tack stores) may be substituted.

Plant this slender-bladed perennial with companions that also like boggy places and clay: *Iris pseudacorus,* astilbes, *Myosotis palustris,* and *Lysimachia nummularia.* Consider swamp magnolia (*Magnolia virginiana*), often called sweet bay magnolia, if a tree is needed in such boggy situations. And always remember that the cattail should be confined!

Try graceful cattail for a practical solution in bare, wet areas of the landscape or just as an oddly pleasant surprise in the garden. Also try it, again in water-tight containers, on the terrace or patio for a privacy screen. It is available from Waterford Gardens.

Typha angustifolia
(ti'fa ang-gus-ti-fol'ee-a)
GRACEFUL CATTAIL

Veronica 'Sunny Border Blue', still blooming in September.

On the right is Veronica spicata, *with coralbells on the left and baby's breath in the back.*

॰๛

Speedwell . . . I don't know how speedy it is, but I do know that, as one of the best blue-flowering perennials, it quickly becomes a favorite. The stems terminate in elongated triangles of clustered blossoms. These deep violet-blue flowers are not difficult to like.

At eighteen inches, the species flops too much, making some of the cultivars more attractive. *V. a.* 'Crater Lake Blue' has long been a favorite. Even though it falls over too, it doesn't have as far to fall at twelve to fifteen inches, and, when it does, turns back up toward the light, making a satisfactory showing of bright delphinium-blue blossoms.

V. 'Sunny Border Blue' has me in its thrall because it begins blooming in early summer and continues until frost. It is not the dark blue of 'Crater Lake', but for a blue perennial to bloom this long is nothing short of miraculous. Then I must not fail to mention its great, strong stems that hold the foliage upright through the season. There is nothing to do but choose a place to plant it; once that is accomplished, the only attention it requires is cutting back the following spring. We can all thank Robert Bennerup of Sunny Border Nurseries for this great perennial.

Full sun or an eastern location will provide veronicas with the light they thrive in. Soil composition should allow good drainage. I have had 'Sunny Border Blue' do well in clay soil that causes me to spit expletives when I dig in it.

In addition to the various shades of blue veronicas, there are some rose-pink ones and some whites. The favored white is *V. spicata* 'Icicle', blooming most of the summer, and although two feet tall, standing upright. 'Red Fox' is fifteen inches tall, rose-pink, and blooms a long time, too.

V. prostrata offers a lower, creeping variety from four to eight inches, good to cover small areas as a ground cover, and to use in the front of a planting. 'Heavenly Blue' has sapphire blossoms to cool any combination of colors.

I tend to plant the varieties of veronica mentioned above because they tend to take care of themselves better than most. Choosing stable perennials will always reduce the work involved.

Try 'Sunny Border Blue' with Russian sage in the background and lamb's-ears 'Silver Carpet' in the front. You can have fun using veronicas, knowing they will improve any chosen color combination.

॰๛

Veronica austriaca
(ve-ron'i-ka au-stri-ah'ka)
SPEEDWELL

201

Resources

BOOKS

Paul Aden, *The Hosta Book* (Portland, Ore.: Timber Press, 1988).

Alan Bloom, *Perennials for Your Garden* (Chicago: Floraprint USA, 1981).

Beth Chatto, *The Damp Garden* (London: Dent, 1982).

Allen J. Coombs, *Dictionary of Plant Names* (Portland, Ore.: Timber Press, 1994).

Diane Heilenman, *Gardening in the Lower Midwest: A Practical Guide for the New Zones 5 and 6* (Bloomington: Indiana University Press, 1994).

Michael Jefferson-Brown, *The Lily* (North Pomfret, Vt.: David & Charles, 1988).

David L. Jones, *Encyclopedia of Ferns* (Portland, Ore.: Timber Press, 1987).

Christopher Lloyd, *Clematis* (Deer Park, Wis.: Capability's Books, 1989).

Tim Morehouse with Frank Clark and Ezra Haggard, *Basic Projects and Plantings for the Garden* (Harrisburg, Pa.: Stackpole Books, 1993).

Russell Page, *The Education of a Gardener* (New York: Random House, 1983).

George Schenk, *The Complete Shade Gardener* (Boston: Houghton Mifflin, 1984).

Steven M. Still, *Manual of Herbaceous Ornamental Plants,* 4th ed. (Champaign, Ill.: Stipes Publishing Co., 1994).

Taylor's *Master Guide to Gardening* (Boston: Houghton-Mifflin, 1994).

Mary E. Wharton and Roger Barbour, *The Wildflowers and Ferns of Kentucky* (Lexington: University Press of Kentucky, 1979).

Donald Wyman, *Wyman's Gardening Encyclopedia* (New York: Macmillan, 1977).

Peter F. Yeo, *Hardy Geraniums* (Portland, Ore.: Timber Press, 1985).

NURSERIES (MAIL ORDER AND OTHERWISE)

Akin' Back Farm, LaGrange, KY, 502/222–5791: Perennials, herbs, hostas, daylilies

Kurt Bluemel, 2543 Hess Road, Fallston, MD 21047: Perennials and grasses

Bluestone Perennials, 7211 Middle Ridge Road, Madison, OH 44057–3096, 800/852–5243: Small, inexpensive perennials

Burnham Woods Nursery, Bloomington, IN 47408: Perennials, hostas, iris, daylilies

Burpee, 300 Park Avenue, Warminster, PA 18991–0001, 800/888–1447: Perennials, herbs, wildflowers, seeds

Busse Gardens, 13579 10th St. NW, Cokato, MN 55321–9426, 800/544–3192: Perennials

Carroll Gardens, Inc., P.O. Box 310, Westminster, MD 21158, 410/848–5422: Perennials

Dutch Gardens, P.O. Box 200, Adelphia, NJ 07710: Hardy and tender bulbs and a few perennials

Heronswood Nursery Ltd., 7530 238th Street NE, Kingston, WA 98346: Trees, shrubs, perennials, grasses

The Iris Garden, Route 1, Box CW21, Spencer, IN 47460: Bearded and Siberian iris

Klehm Nursery, Champaign, IL, 800/553–3715: Perennials, hostas, daylilies, peonies

The Landscape Supply, 2435 Burlington Pike, Burlington, KY 41005: Perennials, grasses, hostas, shrubs, daylilies

Louie Hillenmeyer Flower Power Shop, 344 Romany Road, Lexington, KY 40502, 606/266–9843: Perennials

Margaret's Garden (prop. Margaret McDonough), Courtstreet Market, Cincinnati, OH 45220, 513/385–8274: Perennials

Michler Florist, 417 East Maxwell Street, Lexington, KY 40508, 606/254–0383: Perennials

Pinecliffe Daylily Gardens, 6604 Scottsville Rd., Floyds Knobs, IN 47119: Daylilies

Soules Garden, 5809 Rahke Rd., Indianapolis, IN 46217: Hostas, daylilies, companion plants

Springbrook Gardens, Inc., 6776 Heisley Road, P.O. Box 388, Mentor, Ohio 44061–0388: Perennials

K. Van Bourgondien & Sons, Inc., P.O. Box 1000 Route 109, Babylon, NY 11702–0598: Perennials

Waterford Gardens, Saddle River, NJ 07458, 201/327–0721: Water plants, fish, pools

Wayside Gardens, Hodges, SC 29695–0001, 800/845–1124: Perennials, shrubs, trees, bulbs

Wyle Wynde Nursery (Slade's Iris) R. 2, Box 84, Cynthiana, KY 41031: Iris, Siberian iris, perennials

MISCELLANEOUS

American Hemerocallis Society, Display Gardens Chairman, Dan Trimmer, 56 Winding Way, Water Mill, NY 11976, 516/726–9640.

Index

Ezra Haggard is more than a garden designer: he is an artist who works with, knows, and loves plants. His twenty years of horticultural experience in the Lower Midwest amply qualify him to give advice on helping to make our gardens more beautiful and interesting and our gardening lives easier.

He is co-author with Tim Morehouse and Frank Clark of *Basic Projects and Plantings for the Garden*. His base of operations is Lexington, Kentucky.